Congressional Research Service

African American Members of the United States Congress: 1870-2012

Jennifer E. Manning
Information Research Specialist

Colleen J. Shogan
Deputy Director and Senior Specialist

November 26, 2012

Congressional Research Service

7-5700

www.crs.gov

RL30378

Summary

There are 43 African American Members serving in the 112th Congress, all in the House of Representatives. There have been 133 African American Members of Congress: 127 have been elected to the House; 5 have been elected to the Senate; and 1 has been appointed to the Senate. There have been 104 Democrats, 101 in the House and 3 in the Senate; and 29 Republicans, 26 in the House and 3 in the Senate.

The number of African American Members has steadily increased since the first African Americans entered Congress in 1870. There were fewer than 10 Members until the 91st Congress (1969-1971). In the 98th Congress (1983-1985), the number surpassed 20 for the first time and then jumped to 40 in the 103rd Congress (1993-1995). Since the 106th Congress (1999-2001), the number has remained between 39 and 44 serving at any one time.

The first African American Member of Congress was Hiram Rhodes Revels (R-MS), who served in the Senate in the 41st Congress (served 1870-1871). The first African American Member of the House was Joseph H. Rainey (R-SC), who also served in the 41st Congress.

Shirley Chisholm (D-NY), elected to the 91st through 97th Congresses (1969-1983), was the first African American woman in Congress. Since that time, 30 other African American women have been elected, including Senator Carol Moseley-Braun (D-IL, 1993-1999), who is the only African American woman, as well as the first African American Democrat, elected to the Senate.

Representative John Conyers, Jr. (D-MI, 1965-present), the current chair of the House Judiciary Committee, holds the record for length of service by an African American Member (46 years). He was first elected to the 89th Congress (1965-1967) and has served since January 3, 1965.

Representative James E. Clyburn (D-SC, 1993-present) and former Representatives William H. Gray III (D-PA, 1979-1991) and J.C. Watts (R-OK, 1995-2003) have been elected to the highest leadership positions held by African American Members of Congress. Representative Clyburn, the House Assistant Democratic leader in the 112th Congress, served as the House majority whip in the 110th and 111th Congresses and as vice chair of the House Democratic Caucus in the 108th and 109th Congresses. Representative Gray was chair of the House Democratic Caucus in 1989 (101st Congress). Later in that Congress, when a vacancy occurred, he was elected House majority whip, a position he held until his resignation from Congress in September 1991 (102nd Congress). Representative Watts served as chair of the House Republican Conference in the 106th-107th Congresses (1997-2001).

Twenty African Americans have served as committee chairs, 19 in the House and 1 in the Senate.

The Congressional Black Caucus (CBC), whose origins date back to 1969, currently has 43 members. Over its 40-year history, the CBC has been one of the most influential caucuses in Congress.

This report will be updated as needed.

Contents

Figures

Tables

Contacts

Introduction

One hundred thirty-three African Americans have served in the U.S. Congress: 127 in the House and 6 in the Senate.[1] Of these, 31 have been women. A record 43 African American Members (all in the House, including two delegates) serve in the 112th Congress. All but 2 are Democrats and 15 are women. No African Americans have served in both houses of Congress.

The majority of African American Members of Congress (103) have been Democrats; 29 have been Republicans. Five others, all Democrats, have served as Delegates to the House. All of the Democrats have been elected in the 20th and 21st centuries. Twenty-two African American Republicans served in the 19th century House, five in the 20th century (four in the House and one in the Senate), and one was reelected to a single term in the 21st century before retiring. Two others have been elected to the House in the 21st century.

Historical Overview of African Americans in Congress

Excluding delegates, African Americans currently hold 41 (9.4%) of the 435 voting seats in the House of Representatives in the 112th Congress. Including delegates, African Americans currently hold 43 seats in the House of Representatives, totaling 9.8% of the entire House.[2] No African Americans serve in the Senate in the 112th Congress.

---

[1] Includes three Delegates from the U.S. Virgin Islands and two from the District of Columbia. For an in-depth look at African Americans in Congress, refer to U.S. Congress, House, Office of History and Preservation, *Black Americans in Congress, 1870-2007* (Washington: GPO, 2008), http://baic.house.gov .

[2] 44 African Americans were elected to the House at the beginning of the 112th Congress; one African American Member died in March 2012 and was replaced by another African American Member in November 2012, and another resigned in November 2012.

Figure 1. Trends in the Number of African Americans in Congress, 41st Congress (1870-1871) to Present

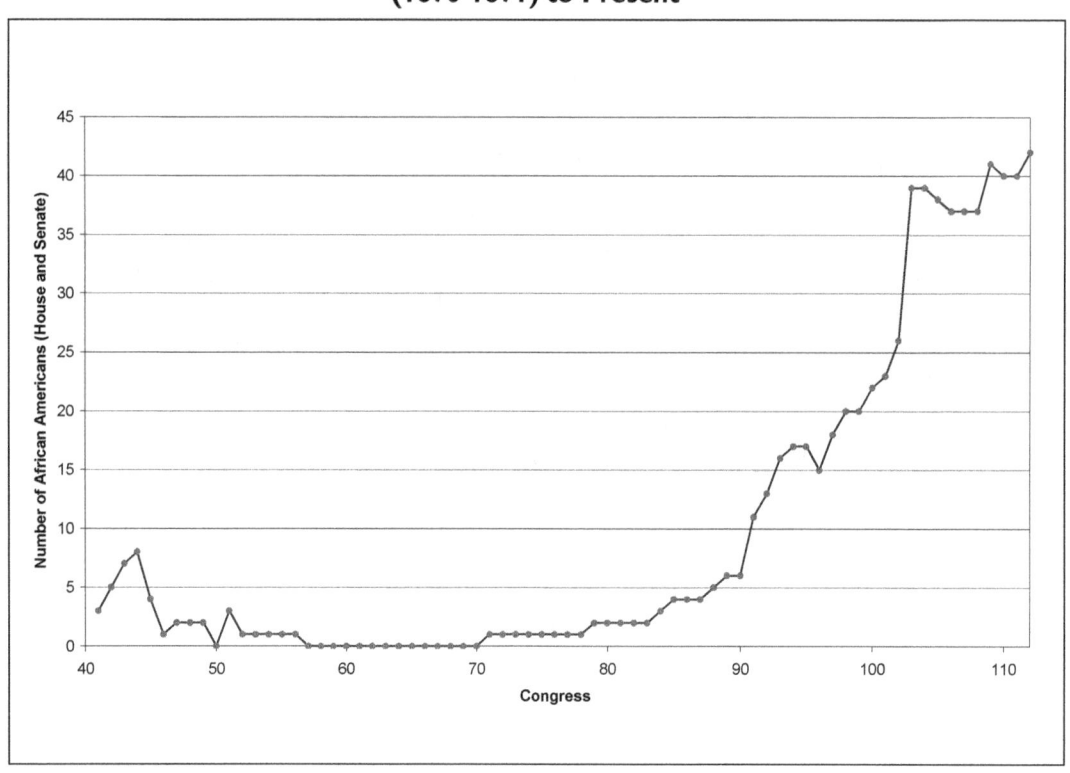

Source: *Black Americans in Congress, 1870-2007* (Washington: GPO, 2008), http://baic.house.gov, supplemented by CRS.

Note: Delegates are not included in the data.

As **Figure 1** shows, the number of African Americans serving in Congress stayed below 10 until the 91st Congress (1969-1971), when those in the House doubled, growing from 5 to 10 in one Congress. The number of African-American Senators remained at 1. Subsequently, the number of African American Members steadily increased. In the 98th Congress (1983-1985), the number surpassed 20 for the first time and in the 103rd Congress (1993-1995) reached 40. Since the 106th Congress (1999-2001), the number has remained between 39 and 44 at any one time.

Figure 2. African Americans in Congress

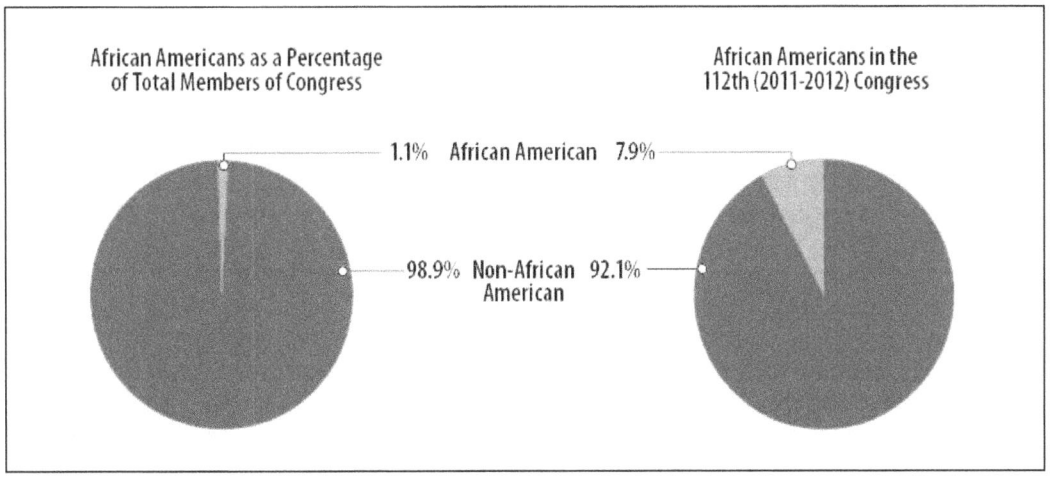

African Americans as a Percentage of Total Members of Congress

African Americans in the 112th (2011-2012) Congress

1.1%   African American   7.9%

98.9%   Non-African   92.1%
American

Source: *Black Americans in Congress, 1870-2007* (Washington: GPO, 2008), http://baic.house.gov, supplemented by CRS. Figures compiled by CRS.

Notes: Delegates are not included in the data.

African Americans did not serve in Congress until the 41st Congress (1869-1871) when two were elected to the House and a third, Hiram Rhodes Revels (R-MS), was elected to the Senate by the Mississippi state legislature.[3] This was during the Reconstruction period following the Civil War (1865-1877). Of particular significance is the fact that "all of the 17 African-American Members between 1870 and 1887 came from the new Reconstruction governments in the former Confederacy."[4] No African Americans served in Congress from the 57th Congress (1901-1903) until the 71st Congress (1929-1931), when one Member was elected to the House. This was in part because (1) the congressional focus on racial equality had faded; (2) the slow disintegration of the Republican-dominated Reconstruction governments had a detrimental effect on the rights of black voters, and those seeking political office were vulnerable to Democratic state governments controlled by former Confederates and their sympathizers; (3) a variety of impediments such as the poll tax and educational tests prevented African Americans from voting; and (4) some state legislatures attempted to gerrymander congressional districts to restrict the election of African Americans.[5]

Despite increases in the number of African Americans serving in Congress, especially since the 91st Congress (1969-1971), **Figure 2** shows that 1.1% of Members in the United States history have been African Americans. **Figure 2** shows the current composition of the 112th Congress with 7.9% voting African American Members.

---

[3] This was prior to the ratification of the Seventeenth Amendment to the Constitution in 1913 that provided for the direct election of Senators.

[4] U .S. Congress, House, Office of History and Preservation, *Black Americans in Congress, 1870-2007* (Washington: GPO, 2008), p. 22; and http://baic.house.gov.

[5] Ibid., pp. 152-159.

African American Firsts in Congress

The first African American Member of Congress was Hiram Rhodes Revels (R-MS), who served in the Senate in the 41ˢᵗ Congress (1870-1871). He also has the distinction of being the first African American Member of the Senate and the first African American Member of Congress from Mississippi. On January 20, 1870, he was chosen by the Mississippi legislature to take the seat previously held by Albert G. Brown, who withdrew from the Senate on January 12, 1861, after Mississippi seceded from the Union. Senator Blanche K. Bruce (R-MS, 1875-1881) was the first African American Senator to serve a full Senate term of six years.

Joseph H. Rainey (R-SC, 1870-1879) was the first African American Member of the House of Representatives, beginning service, like Senator Revels, in the 41ˢᵗ Congress. Shirley Chisholm (D-NY), elected to the 91ˢᵗ through 97ᵗʰ Congresses (1969-1983), was the first African American woman to serve in Congress. Edward Brooke (R-MA) was the first African American elected to the Senate after passage of the Seventeenth Amendment, which provided for the direct election of Senators. He served in the 90ᵗʰ through 95ᵗʰ Congresses (1967-1979).

Carol Moseley-Braun (D-IL, 1993-1999) is the only African American woman, as well as the first African American Democrat, to serve in the Senate. President Barack Obama was the first African American male Democrat to serve in the Senate. He served as a Senator from Illinois from 2005 until his resignation on November 16, 2008, after he was elected President of the United States. Senator Roland Burris (D-IL, 2009-present), who was appointed to the seat vacated by President Obama, is the first African American appointed to the Senate. Representative Walter Fauntroy (D-DC, 1971-1991) was the first African American delegate to serve in Congress.

Representative Charles Diggs (D-MI, 1955-1980) was the first chair of the Congressional Black Caucus.

As chair of the Senate Select Committee to Investigate Freedman's Savings and Trust Company (46ᵗʰ Congress), Blanche K. Bruce (R-MS) was the first African American to chair a congressional committee. As chair of the House Committee on Expenditures in the Executive Departments (81ˢᵗ Congress), William L. Dawson (D-IL, 1943-1970) was the first African American to chair a House committee.

Length of Service

John Conyers Jr. (D-MI), the current chair of the House Judiciary Committee, has served longer than any other African American Member of Congress. Representative Conyers has served since 1965. Edward Brooke (R-MA, 1967-1979) holds the record for Senate service by an African American.

How African Americans Enter Congress

Article I, Section 2 of the United States Constitution requires that all Members of the House of Representatives must be "chosen every second Year by the People of the several States." Therefore, all Representatives enter office through election, even those who enter after a seat becomes open during a Congress. By contrast, the Seventeenth Amendment gives state legislatures the option to empower governors to fill Senate vacancies by temporary appointment.

All 126 of the African Americans who have served in the House have been elected, as well as all but one of the six African American Senators. The lone exception is Senator Roland Burris (D-IL, 2009-2010).

African American Members in Leadership Positions

Representative James E. Clyburn (D-SC, 1993-present), the House assistant minority leader in the 112th Congress, served as the House majority whip in the 110th-111th Congresses, and as vice chair of the House Democratic Caucus in the 108th and 109th Congresses. Former Representatives William H. Gray III (D-PA, 1979-1991) and J.C. Watts (R-OK, 1995-2003) were also elected members of the House leadership. Representative Gray was chair of the House Democratic Caucus in 1989 (101st Congress). Later in that Congress, when a vacancy occurred, he was elected House majority whip, a position he held until his resignation from Congress in September 1991 (102nd Congress). Representative Watts served as chair of the House Republican Conference in the 106th-107th Congresses (1997-2003).

Representative John Lewis (D-GA, 1987-present), the Democratic senior chief deputy whip in the 110th-112th Congresses, served as a Democratic chief deputy whip in the 102nd-109th Congresses (1991-2007). Representative Maxine Waters (D-CA, 1991-present) has served as a Democratic chief deputy whip since the 106th Congress, and Representative G.K. Butterfield (D-NC, 2004-present) has served as a Democratic chief deputy whip since the 110th Congress. Former Representative Shirley Chisholm (D-NY, 1969-1983) served as secretary to the Democratic Caucus in the 96th Congress (1977-1979).

Nineteen African American Representatives and one Senator have chaired congressional committees, including four in the House in the 111th Congress and a record five in the 110th Congress. No African Americans serve as committee chairs in the 112th Congress.

The other African American committee chairs were Senator Blanche Bruce (R-MS, 1875-1881) and Representatives Yvonne B. Burke (D-CA, 1973-1979); William L. Clay Sr. (D-MO, 1969-2001); William L. Dawson (D-IL, 1943-1970); Ronald V. Dellums (D-CA, 1971-1998); Charles C. Diggs Jr. (D-MI, 1955-1980); Julian Dixon (D-CA, 1979-2000); William H. Gray III (D-PA, 1979-1991); Augustus F. Hawkins (D-CA, 1963-1991); George T. (Mickey) Leland (D-TX, 1979-1989); Parren J. Mitchell (D-MD, 1971-1987); Robert N.C. Nix Sr. (D-PA, 1958-1979); Adam Clayton Powell Jr. (D-NY, 1945-1967, 1969-1971); Louis Stokes (D-OH, 1969-1999); Juanita Millender-McDonald (D-CA, 1996-2007); and Stephanie Tubbs Jones (D-OH, 1999-2008).[6]

Congressional Black Caucus

The Congressional Black Caucus (CBC) traces its origins to the start of the 91st Congress in January 1969 when Representative Charles Diggs (MI) brought together the other African American Members of the House to form the Democratic Select Committee.[7] As the Select

---

[6] For more information, refer to "Black Americans Who Have Chaired Congressional Committees, 1870 to Present" at the *Black Americans in Congress* website at http://baic.house.gov/historical-data/congressional-committee-chairs.html

[7] James Stuart Olson, "Congressional Black Caucus," in *Historical Dictionary of the 1970s*, ed. James Stuart Olson (Santa Barbara, CA: Greenwood Publishing Group, 1999), p. 103; and Congressional Black Caucus Foundation, Inc., (continued...)

Committee expanded its legislative goals and activities during 1970, it reorganized into a more formal organization, the Congressional Black Caucus, with 13 members at the start of the 92nd Congress in 1971. The CBC became only the fifth Member organization to exist in Congress.[8] Since the 92nd Congress, all African American Members except three have joined the CBC. Currently, there are 42 members of the Congressional Black Caucus, comprising all the African American Members of Congress except one. It is chaired by Representative Emanuel Cleaver (MO).[9]

Three main factors contributed to the founding of the CBC: greater African American participation in electoral politics following passage of the 1965 Voting Rights Act, a perceived African American leadership vacuum due to the deaths or marginalization of many civil rights leaders in the late 1960s, and perceived inattention to issues of concern to African Americans by the Nixon Administration.[10] Although the number of African American legislators increased during the 1968 and 1970 congressional elections, the African American community was still proportionally underrepresented in Congress. According to the CBC, its founding members "believed that a black caucus in Congress, speaking with a single voice, would provide political influence and visibility far beyond their numbers."[11]

In addition to serving as a voice for the African American community, the Congressional Black Caucus has also addressed issues of concern to the poor and other underrepresented minority groups, both in the United States and abroad. This broader scope is reflected in the original mission of the CBC: "to promote the public welfare through legislation designed to meet the needs of millions of neglected citizens."[12] In domestic policy, the CBC has supported efforts to improve access and quality of education and health care, reduce unemployment, protect voting rights, and provide better housing and childcare for the poor and working class. In foreign policy, the CBC generally supports international human rights and focuses on issues where current U.S. policy may conflict with professed American values of liberty and equality.[13] This was shown in the CBC stance against apartheid in South Africa, its push for humanitarian aid and refugee assistance for Haiti, and the continual efforts of some CBC members to urge Congress to consider the concerns of the Palestine Liberation Organization (PLO).[14] Historically, the CBC has used

---

(...continued)

"Origins and the History of the Congressional Black Caucus," at http://www.cbcfinc.org/cbc/html.

[8] CRS Report R40683, *Congressional Member Organizations: Their Purpose and Activities, History, and Formation*, by Robert Jay Dilger.

[9] For more information about the current CBC members, see Congressional Black Caucus, "CBC Members," at http://www.house.gov/cleaver/cbc/members.html.

[10] Carol M. Swain, *Black Faces, Black Interests: The Representation of African Americans in Congress* (Lanham, MD: University Press of America, 2006), p. 37; and Charles E. Jones, "An Overview of the Congressional Black Caucus," in *Readings in American Political Issues*, ed. Franklin D. Jones, et al., (Dubuque, IA: Kendall/Hunt Publishing Company, 1987), p. 233.

[11] Congressional Black Caucus, "History & Agenda," at http://thecongressionalblackcaucus.lee.house.gov/history_details.html.

[12] Ibid.

[13] Raymond W. Copson, *The Congressional Black Caucus and Foreign Policy* (New York: Novinka Books, 2003), pp. 14-15.

[14] Swain, *Black Faces, Black Interests: The Representation of African Americans in Congress*, pp. 11-12.

---

both informal and formal strategies to influence foreign policy, varying from organizing protests and boycotts to conducting special hearings, writing letters, and introducing legislation.[15]

At times, the CBC plays an oppositional role, both within Congress and the established party structure. One scholar has argued that within Congress, the CBC serves "not only as an interest group for blacks but also as a labor union for its members."[16] In 1974, for example, House leadership agreed to put one black Member on each major committee at the urging of the CBC.[17] The CBC also often issues declarations of its policy agenda, distinct from either party's agenda. This was reflected by some of the earliest caucus efforts, beginning with a February 1970 letter to President Richard Nixon addressing issues facing black and impoverished Americans and the presentation of 61 policy recommendations to the President concerning domestic and foreign policy matters at a meeting on March 25, 1971.[18] Another example is the CBC alternative federal budget, which has been presented to Congress annually since 1981.[19]

The caucus also plays a symbolic role for the African American community. Some scholars have argued that the caucus is more effective as a social and community organization than it is a political or legislative institution.[20] Evidence also indicates that in recent years CBC members may use the organization's increased size and influence within the House to ascend to party and committee leadership positions.[21] As Members of the House and Senate, CBC members held the highest national elected office positions of any African Americans until the 2008 presidential election of former CBC member Barack Obama. The CBC Foundation (CBCF) sponsors a number of leadership development programs, internships, fellowships, and scholarships to encourage the next generation of African American leaders.[22] In Congress, CBC members regularly celebrate the accomplishments of African Americans and minorities, by introducing resolutions to commemorate African American and minority leaders as well as civil rights activists.[23]

---

[15] Michael L. Clemons, "Conceptualizing the Foreign Affairs Participation of African Americans," in African Americans in Global Affairs: Contemporary Perspectives, ed. Michael L. Clemons, (Boston, MA: Northeastern University Press, 2010), pp. 57-59.

[16] Robert Singh, *The Congressional Black Caucus: Racial Politics in the U.S. Congress* (Thousand Oaks, CA: SAGE Publications, 1998), p. xii.

[17] Swain, *Black Faces, Black Interests: The Representation of African Americans in Congress,* p. 40.

[18] Marguerite Ross Barnett, "The Congressional Black Caucus," *Proceedings of the Academy of Political Science*, vol. 32, no. 1 (1975), p. 35.

[19] Copson, *The Congressional Black Caucus and Foreign Policy,* pp. 12-13; For information on recent CBC alternative budgets, see Office of Representative Bobby Scott, "Congressional Black Caucus FY2010 Budget Substitute Amendment"," April 2009 press release, at http://www.bobbyscott.house.gov/index.php?option=com_content&task= view&id=380&Itemid=89.

[20] Arthur B. Levy and Susan Stoudinger, "Sources of Voting Cues for the Congressional Black Caucus," *Journal of Black Studies,* vol. 7 (1976), pp. 29-46.

[21] Kareem Crayton, "The Changing Face of the Congressional Black Caucus," *Southern California Interdisciplinary Law Journal,* vol. 19 (2009-2010), p. 494.

[22] Members of the CBC established the non-profit and non-partisan Congressional Black Caucus Foundation, Inc. (CBCF) in 1976 to "advance the global black community by developing leaders, informing policy and educating the public." In addition to leadership development programs, the CBCF conducts policy research on economic development, public health, and other pertinent issues for the black community. As a part of its public education goals, the CBCF also holds seminars on these topics, and launched an online archive (Avoice Online) to document the history of African Americans in Congress and the history of the CBC. See Congressional Black Caucus Foundation, Inc., "About CBCF," at http://www.cbcfinc.org/about-cbcf.html.

[23] Swain, *Black Faces, Black Interests: The Representation of African Americans in Congress,* p. 17.

Three noteworthy legislative initiatives championed by the CBC include the establishment of Martin Luther King Jr. Day, sanctions on South Africa to pressure an end to apartheid, and humanitarian assistance to Haiti.[24] The subsequent section describes the CBC's role in these legislative endeavors.

Martin Luther King Jr. Day

The bill to establish a federal holiday to honor Dr. Martin Luther King Jr. was signed into law by President Ronald Reagan on November 3, 1983.[25] Representative John Conyers (MI) introduced the first Martin Luther King Jr. holiday bill on April 8, 1968, four days after King's assassination. After its founding in 1971, the CBC became a strong advocate for a Martin Luther King Jr. holiday, frequently participating in demonstrations, orchestrating petition drives, and introducing legislation. In 1971, Congress received a petition signed by 6 million Americans in support of the King holiday, and Representative Conyers and Representative Shirley Chisholm (NY), another CBC member, reintroduced King holiday legislation during every subsequent session of Congress until the holiday became law. On January 15, 1981, musician Stevie Wonder, with the support of the CBC, sponsored a march, rally, and benefit concert in Washington, DC, to celebrate what would have been King's 52nd birthday and to raise awareness about the King holiday legislation.[26]

On August 27, 1983, more than 200,000 people gathered for a civil rights march at the Lincoln Memorial to commemorate the 20th anniversary of King's march on Washington.[27] The attention to King's legacy, coupled with political protests and the spread of local and state King holiday legislation, made 1983 an opportune time for enactment of the Martin Luther King Jr. holiday. The successful 1983 legislation was introduced by CBC member Representative Katie Hall on July 29, passing the House by a vote of 338-90 on August 2 and the Senate by a vote of 78-22 on October 19, and was signed into law on November 2.[28]

Ending Apartheid in South Africa

The CBC began to address apartheid during the 1970s because it felt that the executive branch had not made ending discrimination in South Africa a priority.[29] Between 1972 and 1986,

---

[24] Sources detailing CBC involvement with the Martin Luther King, Jr., Holiday Bill, include Avoice Online, "The Martin Luther King, Jr. Holiday Bill," at http://www.avoiceonline.org/mlk/timeline.html; Jones, "An Overview of the Congressional Black Caucus," p. 236; and Singh, *The Congressional Black Caucus: Racial Politics in the U.S. Congress,* pp. 95-96. For CBC efforts to end apartheid in South Africa, see Avoice Online, "Anti-Apartheid," at http://www.avoiceonline.org/aam/; Copson, *The Congressional Black Caucus and Foreign Policy,* pp. 11-14, pp. 26-30; and Swain, *Black Faces, Black Interests: The Representation of African Americans in Congress,* p. 12. Sources detailing CBC involvement with humanitarian aid and other policies regarding Haiti include Copson, *The Congressional Black Caucus and Foreign Policy,* pp. 37-40; Singh, *The Congressional Black Caucus: Racial Politics in the U.S. Congress,*pp. 188-189; and Swain, *Black Faces, Black Interests: The Representation of African Americans in Congress,* pp. 236-237.

[25] P.L. 98-144, 97 Stat. 917 (Nov. 3, 1983).

[26] Avoice Online, "The Martin Luther King, Jr. Holiday Bill," http://www.avoiceonline.org/mlk/timeline.html.

[27] John Herbers, "1983 March: Left Revives," *New York Times,* August 29, 1983, at http://www.factiva.com.

[28] Congressional Black Caucus, "1983 Legislative Achievements," at http://www.avoiceonline.org/assets/txu-gwc-84-98-f8-01/txu-gwc-84-98-f8-01.pdf; Avoice Online, "Origins of the CBC," at http://www.avoiceonline.org/cbc/history.html; and Swain, *Black Faces, Black Interests: The Representation of African Americans in Congress,* p. 132.

[29] Copson, *The Congressional Black Caucus and Foreign Policy,* p. 27.

---

members of the CBC introduced more than 15 bills seeking to end apartheid and racial discrimination practices in South Africa. As a result of the CBC's Black Leadership Conference, the CBC helped establish TransAfrica in 1976, a foreign policy advocacy group designed to raise awareness about African and Caribbean issues. Besides endorsing legislative sanctions, TransAfrica and the CBC also lobbied corporations and universities to divest from South Africa. Through hearings, rallies, and protests in their home districts and in Washington, DC, CBC members increased attention on apartheid in South Africa.[30]

During the 1980s, public awareness and concern about apartheid grew as violence increased in South Africa. By the mid-1980s, the need to address apartheid in South Africa became more pressing and politically feasible. The Comprehensive Anti-Apartheid Act (H.R. 4868), introduced by a CBC member, Representative William H. Gray (PA),[31] included sanctions against South Africa that would not be eased until certain conditions, like the release of political prisoners, were met. The original sanctions in the bill included banning new investments in or loans to South Africa, prohibiting imports of uranium, steel, and coal imports, and removing airport landing rights for South African Airways. An amendment by another CBC member, Representative Ronald Dellums (CA), strengthened the sanctions to include a full trade embargo and complete divestment from South Africa.[32] The bill was vetoed by President Ronald Reagan on September 26, 1986,[33] but was overridden by a House vote of 313 to 83 on September 29, 1986, and by a Senate vote of 78 to 21 on October 2, 1986.[34]

Humanitarian Aid to Haiti

In 1976, Representative Shirley Chisholm (NY) and Delegate Walter Fauntroy (DC) formed the Congressional Black Caucus Task Force on Haitian Refugees to pursue humane treatment and equal justice for refugees from Haiti entering the United States. The name of the caucus was changed to the Congressional Task Force on Haiti in 1981 as it adopted broader policy objectives regarding Haiti and also included members outside of the CBC.[35]

By 1985, it was clear that the 30-year dictatorial regime of Francois Duvalier and his son Jean-Claude Duvalier was nearing its end. In 1986, the U.S. Embassy, working with the Roman Catholic Church and Haitian army, deposed President Jean-Claude Duvalier peacefully, and Haiti scheduled its first free election for November 29, 1987.[36] In response to the efforts of the

---

[30] For more information about the CBC and the formation of Transafrica, see Avoice Online, "Origins of the CBC," at http://www.avoiceonline.org/cbc/history.html; and TransAfrica Forum, "Our History," at http://www.transafricaforum.org/about-us/our-history. For more information regarding CBC opposition to South African apartheid, see Avoice Online, "Anti-Apartheid," at http://www.avoiceonline.org/aam/.

[31] P.L. 99-440, 100 Stat. 1086 (Oct. 2, 1986).

[32] Copson, *The Congressional Black Caucus and Foreign Policy,* pp. 26-30.

[33] Pres. Ronald Reagan, "Anti-Apartheid Act of 1986 – Veto Message from the President of the United States," read in the House, *Congressional Record*, vol. 132, part 19 (September 29, 1986), pp. 27076-27077.

[34] "Roll Call 425," *Congressional Record*, vol. 132, part 19 (September 29, 1986), p. 27101; and "Roll Call 311," *Congressional Record*, vol. 132, part 19 (October 2, 1986), p. 27859.

[35] Copson, *The Congressional Black Caucus and Foreign Policy,* p. 13.

[36] Walter E. Fauntroy, "Haiti Doesn't Need a Tarzan to Come Rescue It," letter to the editor, *New York Times*, September 16, 1987.

Congressional Task Force on Haiti, American aid to Haiti doubled from $50 million in 1986 to $101 million in 1987, despite tight fiscal conditions.[37]

CBC activism for Haiti continued during the late 1980s and 1990s, as a series of military coups led to a difficult post-Duvalier transition period. After Haiti's first democratic presidential election in December 1990, President Bertrand Aristide was overthrown in September 1991, eight months after taking office. Many in the CBC believed the only remedy for the escalating refugee crisis was to restore Aristide to office. Beginning in October 1993, the CBC asked President Bill Clinton to impose the strongest military sanctions available against Haiti or to conduct a military intervention. A letter sent to President Clinton on March 18, 1994, by the CBC and signed by all its members, stated that "The United States Haiti policy must be scrapped." The CBC supported the U.S.- and U.N.-imposed sanctions on Haiti during May and June 1994, with some members advocating for even stronger sanctions. An envoy sent to Haiti on September 18, 1994, by President Clinton convinced Haiti's military rulers to resign and to allow U.S. peacekeeping troops to enter the country and restore Aristide to the presidency.[38]

Concerned about the cost of the Haiti mission and the lack of a troop withdrawal date, Representative Gary Franks (CT), the only Republican member of the CBC, publicly opposed the Clinton Administration's policy and blamed the CBC for the President's decision, stating that a "majority of the Congressional Black Caucus wanted the United States to invade Haiti, and President Clinton caved in." Others argue that Clinton and the CBC simply shared the same position and that the refugee situation constituted a vital American interest.[39]

Tables and Data

This section of the report provides tabular information on African American Members of Congress, including the Congresses in which they served, the committees, on which they served, and an indication of the committees they chaired or co-chaired, or served as ranking Member. In addition, five tables summarize information about African American Members.

Table 1 presents the number and names of African American Members by Congress. **Table 2** presents the same information by state. **Table 3** shows the changing number of African American Members serving in Congress since 1870, when the first Member was elected.

Most of the data presented are drawn from the *Biographical Directory of the American Congress*, http://bioguide.congress.gov, various editions of the *Congressional Directory*, and a broad range of Congressional Quarterly Inc. and Leadership Directories Inc. publications. For additional information, refer to *Black Americans in Congress, 1870-2007*, (Washington: GPO, 2008), http://baic.house.gov, written by the Office of History and Preservation in the House of Representatives.[40]

---

[37] David Binder, "Washington Talk: Foreign Affairs; Haitians Gain Influential Following in America," *New York Times*, September 23, 1987, p. A26.

[38] Copson, *The Congressional Black Caucus and Foreign Policy*, pp. 38-39.

[39] Rep. Richard Gephardt et al., "Commending the President and the Special Delegation to Haiti, and Supporting the United States Armed Forces in Haiti," remarks in the House, *Congressional Record*, vol. 140, part 18 (September 19, 1994), pp. 24755-24768.

[40] The *Black Americans in Congress* website, http://baic.house.gov, is updated for each Congress, despite the "2007" in (continued...)

For 112th Congress committee assignments, the sources are *Official Alphabetical List of the Members with Committee Assignments in the 112th Congress* (available online from the clerk's website at http://clerk.house.gov/committee_info/oal.pdf).

Note that the names and jurisdiction of House and Senate committees have changed several times over the years covered by this report. In the interest of brevity, this report does not identify all historical name changes. The committee names that are listed are those that were in effect at the time a particular Member served on a panel.

Alphabetical Listing of African American Members, Selected Biographical Information, and Committee Assignments During Their Tenure in Office

BALLANCE, FRANK W. Jr., a Representative from North Carolina. Born on February 15, 1942. Elected as a Democrat to the 108th Congress; served from January 7, 2003, until his resignation June 11, 2004.

Committee Assignments	Congress
H. Agriculture	108th
H. Small Business	108th

BASS, KAREN, a Representative from California. Born on October 3, 1953. Elected as a Democrat to the 112th Congress; has served since January 3, 2011.

Committee Assignments	Congress
H. Budget	112th
H. Foreign Affairs	112th

BISHOP, SANFORD D. Jr., a Representative from Georgia. Born on February 4, 1947. Elected as a Democrat to the 103rd through 112th Congresses; has served since January 5, 1993.

Committee Assignments	Congress
H. Agriculture	103rd-107th
H. Post Office and Civil Service	103rd
H. Veterans' Affairs	103rd-104th
H. Select Intelligence	105th-107th
H. Appropriations	108th-112th

(...continued)
the title.

BLACKWELL, LUCIEN E., a Representative from Pennsylvania. Born on August 1, 1931; died on January 24, 2003. Elected as a Democrat to the 102nd Congress to fill the vacancy caused by the resignation of Representative William Gray; reelected to the 103rd Congress; served from November 11, 1991, to January 3, 1995.

Committee Assignments	Congress
H. Merchant Marine and Fisheries	102nd
H. Public Works and Transportation	102nd-103rd
H. Budget	103rd

BROOKE, EDWARD W., a Senator from Massachusetts. Born on October 26, 1919. Elected as a Republican to two six-year terms beginning with the 90th Congress and served through the 95th Congress, from January 3, 1967, to January 3, 1979. First African American Member of Congress from Massachusetts.

Committee Assignments	Congress
S. Aeronautical and Space Sciences	90th
S. Banking and Currency (ranking Member, 95th)	90th-91st
S. Government Operations	90th
S. Armed Services	91st
S. Select Equal Education Opportunity	91st-92nd
S. Appropriations	92nd-95th
S. Banking, Housing, and Urban Affairs	92nd-95th
S. Special Aging	92nd-95th
S. Select Standards and Conduct	93rd-94th
Jt. Bicentennial Arrangements (vice-chair, 94th)	94th
Jt. Defense Production	94th-95th

BROWN, CORRINE, a Representative from Florida. Born on November 11, 1946. Elected as a Democrat to the 103rd through 112th Congresses; has served since January 5, 1993.

Committee Assignments	Congress
H. Government Operations	103rd
H. Public Works and Transportation	103rd
H. Veterans' Affairs	103rd-112th
H. Transportation and Infrastructure	104th-112th

BRUCE, BLANCHE K., a Senator from Mississippi. Born on March 1, 1841; died on March 17, 1898. Elected as a Republican to a six-year term beginning with the 44th Congress and served through the 46th Congress, from March 4, 1875, to March 3, 1881.

Committee Assignments	Congress
S. Manufactures	44th
S. Pensions	44th-45th
S. Education and Labor	44th-46th
S. Select Mississippi River	45th-46th
S. Select To Investigate the Freedman's	46th
Savings and Trust Company (committee chair, 46th)	

BURKE, YVONNE BRAITHWAITE, a Representative from California. Born on October 5, 1932. Elected as a Democrat to the 93rd through 95th Congresses; served from January 3, 1973, to January 3, 1979. First female chair of the Congressional Black Caucus, 94th Congress.

Committee Assignments	Congress
H. Interior and Insular Affairs	93rd
H. Public Works	93rd
H. Appropriations	94th-95th
H. Select Assassinations	94th-95th
H. Select Beauty Shop (committee chair, 94th-95th)	94th-95th

BURRIS, ROLAND, a Senator from Illinois. Born on August 3, 1937. Appointed as a Democrat to fill the vacancy caused by the resignation of President Barack Obama; appointed on December 31, 2008, to the 110th Congress, but not seated until January 15, 2009, in the 111th Congress. Served from January 15, 2009, to November 29, 2010.

Committee Assignments	Congress
S. Armed Services	111th
S. Homeland Security and Governmental Affairs	111th
S. Veteran's Affairs	111th

BUTTERFIELD, G.K., a Representative from North Carolina. Born on April 27, 1947. Elected as a Democrat to the 108th Congress to fill the vacancy caused by the resignation of Representative Frank Ballance; reelected to the 109th-112th Congresses, has served since July 21, 2004; a chief deputy Democratic whip in the 110th and 112th Congresses.

Committee Assignments	Congress
H. Small Business	108th
H. Agriculture	108th-109th

Committee Assignments	Congress
H. Armed Services	109th
H. Energy and Commerce	110th-112th
H. Standards of Official Conduct	111th

CAIN, RICHARD H., a Representative from South Carolina. Born on April 12, 1825; died on January 18, 1887. Elected as a Republican to the 43rd and 45th Congresses; served from March 4, 1873, to March 3, 1875, and from March 4, 1877, to March 3, 1879.

Committee Assignments	Congress
H. Agriculture	43rd
H. Private Land Claims	45th

CARSON, ANDRÉ, a Representative from Indiana. Born on October 16, 1974. Elected as a Democrat to the 110th Congress to fill the vacancy caused by the death of his grandmother, Julia Carson; reelected to the 111th-112th Congresses; has served since March 13, 2008.

Committee Assignments	Congress
H. Financial Services	110th-112th

CARSON, JULIA M., a Representative from Indiana. Born on July 8, 1938; died in office December 15, 2007. Elected as a Democrat to the 105th through 110th Congresses; served from January 9, 1997, to December 15, 2007.

Committee Assignments	Congress
H. Banking and Financial Services	105th-106th
H. Financial Services	107th-110th
H. Veterans' Affairs	105th-107th
H. Transportation and Infrastructure	108th-110th

CHEATHAM, HENRY P., a Representative from North Carolina. Born on December 27, 1857; died on November 29, 1935. Elected as a Republican to the 51st and 52nd Congresses; served from March 4, 1889, to March 3, 1893.

Committee Assignments	Congress
H. Expenditures on Public Buildings	51st-52nd
H. Education	51st-52nd
H. Agriculture	52nd

CHISHOLM, SHIRLEY A., a Representative from New York. Born on November 30, 1924; died on January 1, 2005. Elected as a Democrat to the 91st through 97th Congresses; served from January 3, 1969, to January 3, 1983. First African American woman elected to Congress and first African American female presidential candidate, 1972. Secretary of the Democratic Caucus in the 96th Congress, 1977-1979.

Committee Assignments	Congress
H. Veterans' Affairs	91st-92nd
H. Education and Labor	92nd-94th
H. Rules	95th-97th

CHRISTENSEN, DONNA M., a Delegate from the Virgin Islands. Born on September 19, 1945. Elected as a Democrat to the 105th Congress through 112th Congresses; has served since January 7, 1997. First woman elected from the Virgin Islands.

Committee Assignments	Congress
H. Resources / H. Natural Resources	105th-112th (1st session)
H. Small Business	106th-109th
H. Homeland Security	108th-110th, 112th (1st session)
H. Energy and Commerce	111th-112th

CHRISTIAN-CHRISTENSEN, DONNA and CHRISTIAN-GREEN, DONNA. See CHRISTENSEN, DONNA.

CLARKE, HANSEN H., a Representative from Michigan. Born on March 2, 1957. Elected as a Democrat to 112th Congress; has served since January 3, 2011.

Committee Assignments	Congress
H. Homeland Security	112th
H. Science, Space and Technology	112th

CLARKE, YVETTE D., a Representative from New York. Born on November 21, 1964. Elected as a Democrat to the 110th through 112th Congresses; has served since January 4, 2007.

Committee Assignments	Congress
H. Education and Labor	110th-111th
H. Homeland Security	110th-112th
H. Small Business	110th-112th

CLAY, WILLIAM L. Sr., a Representative from Missouri. Born on April 30, 1931. Elected as a Democrat to the 91st through 106th Congresses; served from January 3, 1969, to January 3, 2001. Succeeded by his son, Representative William Lacy Clay Jr. First African American Member of Congress from Missouri.

Committee Assignments	Congress
H. Education and Labor / Education and the Workforce (ranking Member, 104th-106th)	91st-103rd, 105th-106th
H. Economic and Educational Opportunities	104th
H. Post Office and Civil Service (committee chair, 102nd-103rd)	93rd-103rd
H. Select to Study the Committee System	96th
H. House Administration	99th-103rd
H. Jt. Library	101st

CLAY, WILLIAM LACY Jr., a Representative from Missouri. Born on July 27, 1956; succeeded his father, Representative William L. Clay Sr. Elected as a Democrat to the 107th-112th Congresses; has served since January 3, 2001.

Committee Assignments	Congress
H. Financial Services	107th-112th
H. Government Reform	107th-109th
H. Oversight and Government Reform	110th-112th

CLAYTON, EVA M., a Representative from North Carolina. Born on September 16, 1934. Elected as a Democrat to the 102nd Congress to fill the vacancy caused by the death of Representative Walter Jones; reelected to the 103rd through 107th Congresses; served from November 5, 1992, to January 3, 2003. Co-chair of the House Democratic Policy Committee in the 104th Congress.

Committee Assignments	Congress
H. Agriculture	103rd-107th
H. Small Business	103rd
H. Budget	105th-107th

CLEAVER, EMANUEL II, a Representative from Missouri. Born on October 26, 1944. Elected as Democrat to the 109th-112th Congresses; has served since January 4, 2005. Chair of the Congressional Black Caucus in the 112th Congress.

Committee Assignments	Congress
H. Financial Services	109th-112th
H. Energy Independence and Global Warming	110th-111th
H. Homeland Security	111th

CLYBURN, JAMES E., a Representative from South Carolina. Born on July 21, 1940. Elected as a Democrat to the 103rd through 112th Congresses; has served since January 5, 1993. Chair of the Congressional Black Caucus in the 106th Congress. Vice chair of the House Democratic Caucus in the 108th-109th Congresses; House majority whip in the 110th and 111th Congresses; Assistant Democratic Leader, 112th Congress.

Committee Assignments	Congress
H. Public Works and Transportation	103rd
H. Veterans' Affairs	103rd-105th
H. Transportation and Infrastructure	104th-105th
H. Small Business	104th
H. Appropriations	106th-109th

COLLINS, BARBARA-ROSE, a Representative from Michigan. Born on April 13, 1939. Elected as a Democrat to the 102nd through 104th Congresses; served from January 3, 1991, to January 3, 1997.

Committee Assignments	Congress
H. Public Works and Transportation	102nd-103rd
H. Transportation and Infrastructure	104th
H. Government Operations / H. Government Reform and Oversight	103rd-104th
H. Post Office and Civil Service	102nd-103rd
H. Science, Space, and Technology	102nd
H. Select Children, Youth, and Families	102nd

COLLINS, CARDISS, a Representative from Illinois. Born on September 24, 1931. Elected as a Democrat to the 93rd through 104th Congresses; served from June 7, 1973, to January 3, 1997. First elected to succeed her husband, Representative George Collins. Chair of the Congressional Black Caucus in the 96th Congress.

Committee Assignments	Congress
H. Government Operations / H. Government Reform and Oversight (ranking Member, 104th)	93rd-104rd
H. Public Works	93rd
H. International Relations	94th-95th
H. Foreign Affairs	96th
H. District of Columbia	95th
H. Energy and Commerce	97th-103rd
H. Commerce	104th
H. Select Population	95th
H. Select Narcotics Abuse and Control	96th-102nd

COLLINS, GEORGE W., a Representative from Illinois. Born on March 5, 1926; died on December 8, 1972, in an airplane crash. Elected as a Democrat to the 91st Congress to fill the vacancy by the death of Representative Daniel Ronan; reelected to the 92nd and 93rd Congresses; served from November 16, 1970, to December 8, 1972. Succeeded by his wife, Representative Cardiss Collins.

Committee Assignments	Congress
H. Government Operations	91st-92nd
H. Public Works	92nd

CONYERS, JOHN Jr., a Representative from Michigan. Born on May 16, 1929. Elected as a Democrat to the 89th through 112th Congresses; has served since January 3, 1965.

Committee Assignments	Congress
H. Judiciary (committee chair, 110th-111th; ranking Member, 104th-109th, 112th)	89th-112th
H. Government Operations (committee chair, 101st-103rd)	92nd-103rd
H. Small Business	100th-103rd

CROCKETT, GEORGE W., a Representative from Michigan. Born on August 10, 1909; died on September 7, 1997. Elected as a Democrat to the 96th Congress to fill the vacancy caused by the resignation of Representative Charles Diggs; reelected to the 97th through 101st Congresses; served from November 12, 1980, to January 3, 1991.

Committee Assignments	Congress
H. Foreign Affairs	96th-101st
H. Judiciary	97th-101st
H. Small Business	97th
H. Select Aging	97th-101st

CUMMINGS, ELIJAH E., a Representative from Maryland. Born on January 18, 1951. Elected as a Democrat to the 104th Congress to fill the vacancy caused by the resignation of Representative Kweisi Mfume; reelected to the 105th through 112th Congresses; has served since April 25, 1996. Chair of the Congressional Black Caucus in the 108th Congress.

Committee Assignments	Congress
H. Government Reform and Oversight / H. Government Reform	104th-109th
H. Oversight and Government Reform (ranking Member, 112th)	110th-112th
H. Transportation and Infrastructure	110th-112th
H. Armed Services	110th
Jt. Economic Committee	109th-112th

DAVIS, ARTUR, a Representative from Alabama. Born on October 9, 1967. Elected as a Democrat to the 108th through 111th Congresses; served from January 7, 2003, to January 3, 2011.

Committee Assignments	Congress
H. Budget	108th-109th
H. Financial Services	108th- 109th
H. Judiciary	110th
H. Ways and Means	110th-111th

DAVIS, DANNY K., a Representative from Illinois. Born on September 6, 1941. Elected as a Democrat to the 105th through 112th Congresses; has served since January 7, 1997.

Committee Assignments	Congress
H. Small Business	105th-109th
H. Government Reform and Oversight / H. Government Reform	105th-109th
H. Oversight and Government Reform	110th-112th
H. Education and the Workforce	108th-109th
H. Education and Labor	110th
H. Ways and Means	111th
H. Homeland Security	112th

DAWSON, WILLIAM L., a Representative from Illinois. Born on April 26, 1886; died in office November 9, 1970. Elected as a Democrat to the 78th through 91st Congresses; served from January 3, 1943, to November 9, 1970.

Committee Assignments	Congress
H. Expenditures in the Executive Departments (committee chair, 81st, 82nd)	78th-82nd
H. Government Operations (ranking Member, 83rd; committee chair, 84th-91st)	83rd-91st
H. Coinage, Weights, and Measures	78th-79th
H. Invalid Pensions	78th-79th
H. Insular Affairs	78th-79th
H. Irrigation and Reclamation	78th-79th
H. Interior and Insular Affairs	82nd
H. District of Columbia	84th-91st

DeLARGE, ROBERT C., a Representative from South Carolina. Born on March 15, 1842; died on February 14, 1874. Elected as a Republican to the 42nd Congress; served from March 4, 1871, until January 24, 1873, when his seat was declared vacant after his election was successfully contested by former Representative Christopher C. Bowen.

Committee Assignment	Congress
H. Manufactures	42nd

DELLUMS, RONALD V., a Representative from California. Born on November 25, 1935. Elected as a Democrat to the 92nd through 105th Congresses; served from January 3, 1971, until February 6, 1998, when he resigned from the House. Chair of the Congressional Black Caucus in the 101st Congress. Elected mayor of Oakland in 2006.

Committee Assignments	Congress
H. District of Columbia (committee chair, 96th-102nd)	92nd-103rd
H. Foreign Affairs	92nd
H. Armed Services (committee chair, 103rd)	93rd-103rd
H. National Security (ranking Member, 104th-105th)	104th-105th
H. Post Office and Civil Service	97th-98th
H. Select Intelligence	94th-102nd

DePRIEST, OSCAR S., a Representative from Illinois. Born on March 9, 1871; died on May 12, 1951. Elected as a Republican to the 71st through 73rd Congresses; served from March 4, 1929, to March 3, 1935. First African American Member of Congress from Illinois.

Committee Assignments	Congress
H. Enrolled Bills	71st-73rd
H. Invalid Pensions	71st-73rd
H. Indian Affairs	71st-73rd
H. Post Office and Post Roads	73rd

DIGGS, CHARLES C. Jr., a Representative from Michigan. Born on December 2, 1922; died on August 24, 1998. Elected as a Democrat to the 84th through 96th Congresses; served from January 3, 1955, until his resignation on June 3, 1980. First African American Member of Congress from Michigan and first chair of the Congressional Black Caucus, 92nd Congress.

Committee Assignments	Congress
H. Interior and Insular Affairs	84th-85th
H. Veterans' Affairs	84th-85th
H. Foreign Affairs	86th-93rd
H. International Relations	94th-96th
H. District of Columbia (committee chair, 93rd-95th)	88th-96th

DIXON, JULIAN C., a Representative from California. Born on August 8, 1934; died on December 8, 2000. Elected as a Democrat to the 96th through 106th Congresses; reelected to the 107th Congress, but died before the commencement of the 107th Congress; served from January 3, 1979, until his death. Chair of the Congressional Black Caucus in the 98th Congress.

Committee Assignments	Congress
H. Appropriations	96th-106th
H. Standards of Official Conduct (committee chair, 99th-101st)	98th-101st
H. Select Intelligence (ranking Member, 106th)	103rd-106th

DYMALLY, MERVYN M., a Representative from California. Born on May 12, 1926. Elected as a Democrat to the 97th through 102nd Congresses; served from January 3, 1981, to January 3, 1993. Chair of the Congressional Black Caucus in the 100th Congress.

Committee Assignments	Congress
H. District of Columbia	97th-102nd
H. Foreign Affairs	97th-102nd
H. Science and Technology	97th-98th
H. Post Office and Civil Service	98th-102nd
H. Education and Labor	99th

EDWARDS, DONNA F., a Representative from Maryland. Born on June 28, 1958. Elected as a Democrat to the 110th Congress to fill the vacancy caused by the resignation of Albert Wynn; reelected to the 111th and 112th Congresses; has served since June 19, 2008.

Committee Assignments	Congress
H. Science and Technology / H. Science, Space and Technology	110th-112th
H. Transportation and Infrastructure	110th-112th
H. Ethics	112th

ELLIOTT, ROBERT B., a Representative from South Carolina. Born on August 11, 1842; died on August 9, 1884. Elected as a Republican to the 42nd and 43rd Congresses; served from March 4, 1871, until his resignation on November 1, 1874.

Committee Assignments	Congress
H. Education and Labor	42nd-43rd
H. Militia	43rd

ELLISON, KEITH, a Representative from Minnesota. Born on August 4, 1963. Elected as a Democrat to the 110th through 112th Congresses; has served since January 4, 2007. First African American Member of Congress from Minnesota. First Muslim Member of Congress.

Committee Assignments	Congress
H. Financial Services	110th-112th
H. Judiciary	110th
H. Foreign Affairs	111th

ESPY, ALBERT MICHAEL (MIKE), a Representative from Mississippi. Born on November 28, 1953. Elected as a Democrat to the 100th through 103rd Congresses. Served from January 6, 1987, to January 25, 1993, when he resigned to become secretary of agriculture.

Committee Assignments	Congress
H. Agriculture	100th-102nd
H. Budget	101st-102nd
H. Select Hunger	101st-102nd
Jt. Deficit Reduction	100th

EVANS, MELVYN H., a Delegate from the Virgin Islands. Born on August 7, 1917; died on November 27, 1984. Elected as a Republican to the 96th Congress; served from January 3, 1979, to January 3, 1981. First African American Delegate from the Virgin Islands.

Committee Assignments	Congress
H. Armed Services	96th
H. Interior and Insular Affairs	96th
H. Merchant Marine and Fisheries	96th

FATTAH, CHAKA, a Representative from Pennsylvania. Born on November 21, 1956. Elected as a Democrat to the 104th through 112th Congresses; has served since January 3, 1995.

Committee Assignments	Congress
H. Government Reform and Oversight / H. Government Reform	104th-106th
H. Economic and Educational Opportunities	104th
H. Education and the Workforce	105th-106th
H. Small Business	104th
H. Standards of Official Conduct	105th-106th
H. Administration	106th-107th
Jt. Printing	106th-107th
H. Appropriations	107th-112th

FAUNTROY, WALTER E., a Delegate from the District of Columbia. Born on February 6, 1933. Elected as a Democrat to the 92nd Congress in a special election after the District of Columbia was authorized to elect a delegate to Congress; reelected to the 93rd through 101st Congresses; served from April 19, 1971, to January 3, 1991. First African American Delegate from the District of Columbia. Chair of the Congressional Black Caucus in the 97th Congress.

Committee Assignments	Congress
H. District of Columbia	92nd-101st
H. Banking and Currency / H. Banking, Currency, and Housing	93rd-94th
H. Banking, Finance, and Urban Affairs	95th-101st
H. Select Assassinations	94th-95th
H. Select Narcotics Abuse and Control	98th-101st

FIELDS, CLEO, a Representative from Louisiana. Born on November 22, 1962. Elected as a Democrat to the 103rd and 104th Congresses; served from January 5, 1993, to January 3, 1997. At age 30, he was the youngest Member of the 103rd Congress.

Committee Assignments	Congress
H. Banking, Finance, and Urban Affairs	103rd
H. Banking and Financial Services	104th
H. Small Business	103rd-104th

FLAKE, FLOYD H., a Representative from New York. Born on January 30, 1945. Elected as a Democrat to the 100th through 105th Congresses; served from January 6, 1987, to November 15, 1997, when he resigned from the House.

Committee Assignments	Congress
H. Banking, Finance, and Urban Affairs	100th-103rd
H. Banking and Financial Services	104th-105th
H. Small Business	100th-105th
H. Government Operations	103rd
H. Select Children, Youth, and Families	100th
H. Select Hunger	100th-102nd

FORD, HAROLD E. Sr., a Representative from Tennessee. Born on May 20, 1945. Elected as a Democrat to the 94th through 104th Congresses; served from January 3, 1975, to January 3, 1997. First African American Member of Congress from Tennessee. Succeeded by his son, Harold E. Ford Jr.

Committee Assignments	Congress
H. Veterans' Affairs	94th

Committee Assignments	Congress
H. Banking, Currency, and Housing	94th
H. Ways and Means	94th-104th
H. Select Aging	94th-102nd
H. Select Assassinations	94th-95th

FORD, HAROLD E. Jr., a Representative from Tennessee. Born on May 11, 1970. Elected as a Democrat to the 105th through 109th Congresses; served from January 7, 1997, to January 3, 2007. At age 26, he was the youngest Member of the 105th Congress. Succeeded his father, Harold E. Ford Sr.

Committee Assignments	Congress
H. Education and the Workforce	105th-107th
H. Government Reform and Oversight / H. Government Reform	105th-106th
H. Financial Services	107th-109th
H. Budget	108th-109th

FRANKS, GARY A., a Representative from Connecticut. Born on February 9, 1953. Elected as a Republican to the 102nd through 104th Congresses; served from January 3, 1991, to January 3, 1997. First African American Member of Congress from Connecticut.

Committee Assignments	Congress
H. Armed Services	102nd
H. Small Business	102nd
H. Energy and Commerce	103rd
H. Commerce	104th
H. Select Committee on Aging	102nd

FRAZER, VICTOR O., a Delegate from the U.S. Virgin Islands. Born on May 24, 1943. Elected as a Democrat to the 104th Congress; served from January 3, 1995, to January 3, 1997.

Committee Assignments	Congress
H. International Relations	104th

FUDGE, MARCIA L., a representative from Ohio. Born on October 29, 1952. Elected as Democrat to the 111th Congress and also to the 110th Congress to fill the vacancy caused by the death of Stephanie Tubbs Jones; reelected to the 112th Congress; has served since November 19, 2008.

Committee Assignments	Congress
H. Education and Labor	111th
H. Science and Technology / H. Science, Space and Technology	111th-112th
H. Agriculture	112th

GRAY, WILLIAM H. III, a Representative from Pennsylvania. Born on August 20, 1941. Elected as a Democrat to the 96th through 102nd Congresses; served from January 3, 1979, to September 11, 1991, when he resigned to become president of the United Negro College Fund. Chair of the House Democratic Caucus in the First Session of the 101st Congress; later in that Congress House Democratic whip (through the First Session of the 102nd Congress).

Committee Assignments	Congress
H. Budget (committee chair, 99th-100th)	96th, 98th-100th
H. District of Columbia	96th-102nd
H. Foreign Affairs	96th
H. Appropriations	97th-102nd
H. House Administration	102nd
Jt. Deficit Reduction	100th

GREEN, AL, a Representative from Texas. Born on September 1, 1947. Elected as a Democrat to the 109th through the 112th Congress; has served since January 4, 2005.

Committee Assignments	Congress
H. Financial Services	109th-112th
H. Science	109th
H. Homeland Security	110th-111th
H. Foreign Affairs	111th

HALL, KATIE B., a Representative from Indiana. Born on April 3, 1938. Elected as a Democrat to the 97th Congress to fill the vacancy caused by the death of Representative Adam Benjamin; reelected to the 98th Congress; served from November 29, 1982, to January 3, 1985. First African American Member of Congress from Indiana.

Committee Assignments	Congress
H. Post Office and Civil Service	98th
H. Public Works and Transportation	98th

HARALSON, JEREMIAH, a Representative from Alabama. Born on April 1, 1846, died in 1916. Elected as a Republican to the 44th Congress; served from March 4, 1875, to March 3, 1877.

Committee Assignments	Congress
H. Public Expenditures	44th

HASTINGS, ALCEE L., a Representative from Florida. Born on September 5, 1936. Elected as a Democrat to the 103rd through 112th Congresses; has served since January 5, 1993.

Committee Assignments	Congress
H. Foreign Affairs	103rd
H. International Relations	104th-107th
H. Merchant Marine and Fisheries	103rd
H. Post Office and Civil Service	103rd
H. Science	104th-105th
H. Select Intelligence	106th-111th
H. Rules	107th-112th
H. Standards of Official Conduct	110th

HAWKINS, AUGUSTUS F., a Representative from California. Born on August 31, 1907; died on November 10, 2007. Elected as a Democrat to the 88th through 101st Congresses; served from January 3, 1963, to January 3, 1991. First African American Member of Congress from California.

Committee Assignments	Congress
H. Education and Labor (committee chair, 98th, 2nd sess. 101st)	88th-101st
H. House Administration (committee chair, 97th- 98th, 2nd sess.)	91st-98th
Jt. Committee on Printing (committee chair, 96th, 98th)	95th-98th
Jt. Committee on the Library (committee chair, 97th)	97th-98th
Jt. Economic	97th-101st

HAYES, CHARLES A., a Representative from Illinois. Born on February 17, 1918; died on April 8, 1997. Elected as a Democrat to the 98th Congress to fill the vacancy caused by the resignation of Representative Harold Washington; reelected to the 99th through 102nd Congresses; served from September 12, 1983, to January 3, 1993.

Committee Assignments	Congress
H. Education and Labor	98th-102nd
H. Small Business	98th-101st
H. Post Office and Civil Service	101st-102nd

HILLIARD, EARL F., a Representative from Alabama. Born on April 9, 1942. Elected as a Democrat to the 103rd through 107th Congresses; served from January 5, 1993, to January 3, 2003.

Committee Assignments	Congress
H. Agriculture	103rd-107th
H. Small Business	103rd-104th
H. International Relations	105th-107th

HYMAN, JOHN ADAMS, a Representative from North Carolina. Born on July 23, 1840; died on September 14, 1891. Elected as a Republican to the 44th Congress; served from March 4, 1875, to March 3, 1877. First African American Member of Congress from North Carolina.

Committee Assignments	Congress
H. Manufactures	44th

JACKSON, JESSE L. Jr., a Representative from Illinois. Born on March 11, 1965. Elected as a Democrat to the 104th Congress to fill vacancy caused by the resignation of Representative Melvin Reynolds; reelected to the 105th through 112th Congresses; served from December 14, 1995 to November 21, 2012, when he resigned.

Committee Assignments	Congress
H. Banking and Financial Services	104th-105th
H. Small Business	105th
H. Appropriations	106th-112th

JACKSON LEE, SHEILA, a Representative from Texas. Born on January 12, 1950. Elected as a Democrat to the 104th through 112th Congresses; has served since January 3, 1995.

Committee Assignments	Congress
H. Judiciary	104th-112th
H. Science	104th-109th
H. Homeland Security	108th-112th
H. Foreign Affairs	110th-111th

JEFFERSON, WILLIAM J., a Representative from Louisiana. Born on March 14, 1947. Elected as a Democrat to the 102nd through 110th Congresses; served from January 3, 1991, to January 3, 2009.

Committee Assignments	Congress
H. Education and Labor	102nd
H. Merchant Marine and Fisheries	102nd
H. District of Columbia	103rd

Committee Assignments	Congress
H. Ways and Means	103rd, 105th-109th
H. National Security	104th
H. House Oversight	104th
H. Budget	109th
H. Small Business	110th
Jt. Printing	104th

JOHNSON, EDDIE BERNICE, a Representative from Texas. Born on December 3, 1935. Elected as a Democrat to the 103rd through 112th Congresses; has served since January 5, 1993. Chair of the Congressional Black Caucus in the 107th Congress.

Committee Assignments	Congress
H. Public Works and Transportation	103rd
H. Transportation and Infrastructure	104th-111th
H. Science, Space, and Technology / H. Science and Technology/ H. Science (ranking Member, 112th)	103rd -112th

JOHNSON, HENRY C. (HANK) Jr., a Representative from Georgia. Born on October 2, 1954. Elected as a Democrat to the 110th through 112th Congresses; has served since January 4, 2007.

Committee Assignments	Congress
H. Armed Services	110th-112th
H. Judiciary	110th-112th
H. Small Business	110th

JONES, STEPHANIE TUBBS, a Representative from Ohio. Born on September 10, 1949; died in office August 20, 2008. Elected as a Democrat to the 106th through 110th Congresses; served from January 3, 1999, to August 20, 2008.

Committee Assignments	Congress
H. Banking and Financial Services	106th
H. Financial Services	107th
H. Small Business	106th
H. Standards of Official Conduct (committee chair, 110th)	107th-110th
H. Ways and Means	108th-110th

JORDAN, BARBARA C., a Representative from Texas. Born on February 21, 1936; died on January 17, 1996. Elected as a Democrat to the 93rd through 95th Congresses; served from January 3, 1973, to January 3, 1979. First African American Member of Congress from Texas.

Committee Assignments	Congress
H. Judiciary	93rd-95th
H. Government Operations	94th-95th

KILPATRICK, CAROLYN CHEEKS, a Representative from Michigan. Born on June 25, 1945. Elected as a Democrat to the 105th through 111th Congresses; served from January 7, 1997, to January 3, 2011. Chair of the Congressional Black Caucus in the 110th Congress.

Committee Assignments	Congress
H. Banking and Financial Services	105th
H. House Oversight	105th
Jt. Committee on the Library	105th
H. Appropriations	106th-111th

LANGSTON, JOHN M., a Representative from Virginia. Born on December 14, 1829; died on November 15, 1897. Elected as a Republican to the 51st Congress; served from September 23, 1890, to March 3, 1891, after he successfully contested the election of Edward Venable. First African American Member of Congress from Virginia.

Committee Assignments	Congress
H. Education	51st

LEE, BARBARA, a Representative from California. Born on July 16, 1946. Elected as a Democrat to the 105th Congress to fill the vacancy caused by the resignation of Representative Ronald Dellums; reelected to the 106th through 112th Congresses; has served since April 20, 1998. Chair of the Congressional Black Caucus in the 111th Congress.

Committee Assignments	Congress
H. Banking and Financial Services	105th-106th
H. Financial Services	107th-109th
H. Science	105th
H. International Relations	106th-109th
H. Appropriations	110th -112th
H. Foreign Affairs	111th

LELAND, GEORGE T. (MICKEY), a Representative from Texas. Born on November 27, 1944; died in a airplane crash on August 7, 1989, while touring Ethiopian refugee camps. Elected as a Democrat to the 96th through 101st Congresses; served from January 3, 1979, to August 7, 1989. Chair of the Congressional Black Caucus in the 99th Congress.

Committee Assignments	Congress
H. District of Columbia	96th-99th
H. Interstate and Foreign Commerce	96th-101st
H. Post Office and Civil Service	96th-101st
H. Select Hunger (committee chair, 98th-101st)	98th-101st
H. Select Children, Youth, and Families	98th

LEWIS, JOHN R., a Representative from Georgia. Born on February 19, 1940. Elected as a Democrat to the 100th through 112th Congresses; has served since January 6, 1987. A Democratic chief deputy whip in the 102nd through 109th Congresses; senior chief deputy Democratic whip in the 110th through 112th Congresses.

Committee Assignments	Congress
H. Public Works and Transportation	100th-102nd
H. Interior and Insular Affairs	100th-102nd
H. Select Aging	101st-102nd
H. District of Columbia	103rd
H. Ways and Means	103rd-112th
H. Budget	108th

LONG, JEFFERSON F., a Representative from Georgia. Born on March 3, 1836; died on February 5, 1900. Elected as a Republican to the 41st Congress after the House declared that Representative Samuel Gove was not entitled to his seat; served from January 16, 1871, to March 3, 1871. First African American Member of Congress from Georgia.

Committee Assignments	Congress
None	—

LYNCH, JOHN R., a Representative from Mississippi. Born on September 10, 1847; died on November 2, 1939. Elected as a Republican to the 43rd, 44th, and 47th Congresses; served from March 4, 1873, to March 3, 1877, and from April 29, 1882, to March 3, 1883, after he successfully contested the election of Representative James Chalmers. At age 26, he was the youngest Member of the 43rd Congress. First African American Member of the House of Representatives from Mississippi.

Committee Assignments	Congress
H. Mines and Mining	43rd-44th
H. Militia	47th
H. Education and Labor	47th

MAJETTE, DENISE L., a Representative from Georgia. Born on May 18, 1955. Elected as a Democrat to the 108th Congress; served from January 7, 2003, to January 3, 2005.

Committee Assignments	Congress
H. Budget	108th
H. Education and the Workforce	108th
H. Small Business	108th

McKINNEY, CYNTHIA A., a Representative from Georgia. Born on March 17, 1955. Elected as a Democrat to the 103rd through 107th Congresses; served from January 5, 1993, to January 3, 2003; elected to the 109th Congress; served from January 4, 2005, to January 3, 2007.

Committee Assignments	Congress
H. Agriculture	103rd
H. Foreign Affairs	103rd
H. International Relations	104th-107th
H. Banking and Financial Services	104th-105th
H. National Security	105th
H. Armed Services	106th-107th, 109th
H. Budget	109th

MEEK, CARRIE P., a Representative from Florida. Born on April 29, 1926. Elected as a Democrat to the 103rd through 107th Congresses; served from January 5, 1993, to January 3, 2003. Succeeded by her son, Representative Kendrick Meek.

Committee Assignments	Congress
H. Appropriations	103rd, 105th-107th
H. Budget	104th
H. Government Reform and Oversight	104th

MEEK, KENDRICK, a Representative from Florida. Born on September 6, 1966. Elected to the 108th through 111th Congresses; served from January 7, 2003, to January 3, 2011. Succeeded his mother, Representative Carrie Meek.

Committee Assignments	Congress
H. Armed Services	108th-110th
H. Homeland Security	108th-109th
H. Ways and Means	110th-111th

MEEKS, GREGORY, a Representative from New York. Born on September 25, 1953. Elected as a Democrat to the 105th Congress to fill the vacancy caused by the resignation of Representative Floyd Flake; reelected to the 106th through 112th Congresses; has served since February 5, 1998.

Committee Assignments	Congress
H. Banking and Financial Services	105th-106th
H. Financial Services	107th-112th
H. International Relations	106th-109th
H. Foreign Affairs	110th-112th

METCALFE, RALPH H., a Representative from Illinois. Born on May 30, 1910; died on October 10, 1978. Elected as a Democrat to the 92nd through 95th Congresses; served from January 3, 1971, to October 10, 1978.

Committee Assignments	Congress
H. Interstate and Foreign Commerce	92nd-95th
H. Merchant Marine and Fisheries	92nd-95th
H. Post Office and Civil Service	95th

MFUME, KWEISI, a Representative from Maryland. Born on October 24, 1948. Elected as a Democrat to the 100th through 104th Congresses; served from January 6, 1987, to February 16, 1996, when he resigned to become executive director of the NAACP. Chair of the Congressional Black Caucus in the 103rd Congress. Co-chair of the Democratic Policy Committee in the 104th Congress.

Committee Assignments	Congress
H. Banking, Finance, and Urban Affairs	100th-103rd
H. Banking and Financial Services	104th
H. Small Business	100th-104th
H. Education and Labor	101st
H. Select Narcotics Abuse and Control	101st-102nd
Jt. Economic	102nd-104th

Committee Assignments	Congress
H. Standards of Official Conduct	103rd
H. Select Hunger	100th

MILLENDER-McDONALD, JUANITA, a Representative from California. Born on September 7, 1938; died in office on April 22, 2007. Elected as a Democrat to the 104th Congress to fill the vacancy caused by the resignation of Representative Walter Tucker; reelected to the 105th through 110th Congresses; served from April 16, 1996, to April 22, 2007.

Committee Assignments	Congress
H. Small Business	104th-110th
H. Transportation and Infrastructure	104th-109th
H. Administration (committee chair, 110th,1st sess.; ranking Member 109th)	108th-110th
Jt. Library (committee chair, 110th,1st session)	108th, 110th
Jt. Printing (committee chair, 110th, 1st sess.)	110th

MILLER, THOMAS E., a Representative from South Carolina. Born on June 17, 1849; died on April 8, 1936. Elected as a Republican to the 51st Congress, when he successfully contested the election of William Elliott; served from September 24, 1890, to March 3, 1891.

Committee Assignments	Congress
H. Library of Congress	51st

MITCHELL, ARTHUR W., a Representative from Illinois. Born on December 22, 1883; died on May 9, 1968. Elected as a Democrat to the 74th through 77th Congresses; served from January 3, 1935, to January 3, 1943. First African American Democrat elected to Congress.

Committee Assignments	Congress
H. Post Office and Post Roads	74th-77th

MITCHELL, PARREN J., a Representative from Maryland. Born on April 29, 1922; died May 28, 2007. Elected as a Democrat to the 92nd through 99th Congresses; served from January 3, 1971, to January 3, 1987. First African American Member of Congress from Maryland. Chair of the Congressional Black Caucus in the 95th Congress.

Committee Assignments	Congress
H. Banking and Currency	92nd-93rd
H. Banking, Finance, and Urban Affairs	94th-99th
H. Select Small Business	92nd-93rd
H. Small Business (committee chair, 97th-99th)	94th, 96th-99th
H. Budget	93rd-95th
Jt. Defense Production	94th-95th
Jt. Economic (vice chair, 95th)	95th-99th

MOORE, GWEN, a Representative from Wisconsin. Born on April 18, 1951. Elected as a Democrat to the 109th through 112th Congresses; has served since January 4, 2005. First African American Member of Congress from Wisconsin.

Committee Assignments	Congress
H. Financial Services	109th-112th
H. Small Business	109th-110th
H. Budget	110th-112th

MOSELEY-BRAUN, CAROL, a Senator from Illinois. Born on August 16, 1947. Elected as a Democrat to a six-year term beginning with the 103rd Congress and served from January 5, 1993, to January 3, 1999. First African American woman and African American Democrat to serve in the Senate; candidate for U.S. President in 2004.

Committee Assignments	Congress
S. Banking, Housing, and Urban Affairs	103rd-105th
S. Judiciary	103rd
S. Small Business	103rd
S. Finance	104th-105th
S. Special Aging	104th-105th

MURRAY, GEORGE W., a Representative from South Carolina. Born on September 22, 1853; died on April 21, 1926. Elected as a Republican to the 53rd and 54th Congresses; served from March 4, 1893, to March 3, 1895, and from June 4, 1896, to March 3, 1897 (successfully contested an election).

Committee Assignments	Congress
H. Education	53rd-54th
H. Expenditures in the Treasury Department	54th

NASH, CHARLES E., a Representative from Louisiana. Born on May 23, 1844; died on June 21, 1913. Elected as a Republican to the 44th Congress; served from March 4, 1875, to March 3, 1877. First African American Member of Congress from Louisiana.

Committee Assignment	Congress
H. Education and Labor	44th

NIX, ROBERT N.C. Sr., a Representative from Pennsylvania. Born on August 9, 1905; died on June 22, 1987. Elected as a Democrat to the 85th Congress to fill the vacancy caused by the resignation of Representative Earl Chudoff; reelected to the 86th through 95th Congresses; served from June 4, 1958, to January 3, 1979. First African American Member of Congress from Pennsylvania.

Committee Assignments	Congress
H. Merchant Marine and Fisheries	85th-86th
H. Foreign Affairs	87th-93rd
H. International Relations	94th-95th
H. Veterans' Affairs	85th-86th
H. Post Office and Civil Service (committee chair, 95th)	88th-95th
H. Select Standards and Conduct	89th
H. Crime	91st

NORTON, ELEANOR HOLMES, a Delegate from the District of Columbia. Born on June 13, 1937. Elected as a Democrat to the 102nd through 112th Congresses; has served since January 3, 1991.

Committee Assignments	Congress
H. District of Columbia	102nd-103rd
H. Post Office and Civil Service	102nd-103rd
H. Public Works and Transportation	102nd-103rd
H. Transportation and Infrastructure	104th-112th
H. Government Reform and Oversight / H. Government Reform	104th-109th

Committee Assignments	Congress
H. Oversight and Government Reform	110th-112th
H. Small Business	104th
Jt. Committee on the Organization of Congress	102nd-103rd
H. Homeland Security	108th-111th

OBAMA, BARACK, a Senator from Illinois. Born on August 4, 1961. Elected as a Democrat to a six-year term beginning with the 109th Congress; served from January 4, 2005, until November 16, 2008, when he resigned after being elected first African American President of the United States.

Committee Assignments	Congress
S. Environment and Public Works	109th-110th
S. Foreign Relations	109th-110th
S. Veterans' Affairs	109th-110th
S. Health, Education, Labor, and Pensions	110th
S. Homeland Security and Governmental Affairs	110th

O'HARA, JAMES E., a Representative from North Carolina. Born on February 26, 1844; died on September 15, 1905. Elected as a Republican to the 48th and 49th Congresses; served from March 4, 1883, to March 3, 1887.

Committee Assignments	Congress
H. Mines and Mining	48th
H. Expenditures on Public Buildings	49th
H. Invalid Pensions	49th

OWENS, MAJOR R., a Representative from New York. Born on June 28, 1936. Elected as a Democrat to the 98th through 110th Congresses; served from January 3, 1983, to January 3, 2007.

Committee Assignments	Congress
H. Education and Labor / H. Education and the Workforce	98th-103rd, 105th-109th
H. Economic and Educational Opportunities	104th
H. Government Operations	98th-103rd
H. Government Reform and Oversight / H. Government Reform	104th-109th

PAYNE, DONALD M., a Representative from New Jersey. Born on July 16, 1934; died in office on March 6, 2012. Succeeded by his son, Donald M. Payne, Jr. Elected as a Democrat to the 101st through 112th Congresses; served from January 3, 1989, to March 6, 2012. First African American Member of Congress from New Jersey. Chair of the Congressional Black Caucus in the 104th Congress.

Committee Assignments	Congress
H. Education and Labor / H. Education and the Workforce	101st-103rd, 105th-109th, 111th-112th
H. Economic and Educational Opportunities	104th
H. Foreign Affairs	101st-103rd, 111th-112th
H. International Relations	104th-109th
H. Government Operations	101st-103rd

PAYNE, DONALD M. Jr., a Representative from New Jersey. Born on December 16, 1958. Elected as a Democrat to the 112th Congress to fill the vacancy caused by the death of his father, Representative Donald Payne, Sr.; has served since November 15, 2012.

Committee Assignments	Congress
None yet	

POWELL, ADAM CLAYTON Jr., a Representative from New York. Born on November 29, 1908; died on April 4, 1972. Elected as a Democrat to the 79th through 90th Congresses, but was not seated in the 90th Congress (excluded from that Congress on March 1, 1967). He served from January 3, 1945, to January 3, 1967. In April 1967, he was reelected in a special election to the seat from which he had been excluded, but he did not attempt to take the oath of office. He was reelected to the 91st Congress and served from January 3, 1969, to January 3, 1971. First African American Member of Congress from New York.

Committee Assignments	Congress
H. Indian Affairs	79th
H. Invalid Pensions	79th
H. Labor	79th
H. Education and Labor (committee chair, 87th-89th)	80th-89th, 91st
H. Interior and Insular Affairs	84th-86th

RAINEY, JOSEPH H., a Representative from South Carolina. Born on June 21, 1832; died on August 2, 1887. Elected as a Republican to the 41st Congress when the House declared the seat of Representative Benjamin Whittemore vacant; reelected to the 42nd through 45th Congresses; served from December 12, 1870, to March 3, 1879. First African American Member of the House of Representatives and first African American Member of Congress from South Carolina.

Committee Assignments	Congress
H. Freedmen's Affairs	41st-42nd
H. Indian Affairs	43rd
H. Invalid Pensions	44th-45th
H. Select Celebration of Proposed National Census of 1875	43rd

RANGEL, CHARLES B., a Representative from New York. Born on June 11, 1930. Elected as a Democrat to the 92nd through 112th Congresses; has served since January 3, 1971. Chair of the Congressional Black Caucus in the 94th Congress.

Committee Assignments	Congress
H. Public Works	92nd
H. Science and Astronautics	92nd
H. Judiciary	92nd-93rd
H. District of Columbia	93rd
H. Ways and Means (committee chair, 110th and 111th; ranking Member, 105th-109th)	94th-112th
H. Select Crime	92nd-93rd
H. Select Narcotics Abuse and Control (committee chair, 98th-102nd)	94th-102nd
Jt. Taxation	104th-105th, 111th

RANSIER, ALONZO J., a Representative from South Carolina. Born on January 3, 1834; died on August 17, 1882. Elected as a Republican to the 43rd Congress; served from March 3, 1873, to March 3, 1875.

Committee Assignments	Congress
H. Manufactures	43rd

RAPIER, JAMES T., a Representative from Alabama. Born on November 13, 1837; died on May 31, 1883. Elected as a Republican to the 43rd Congress; served from March 4, 1873, to March 3, 1875.

Committee Assignment	Congress
H. Education and Labor	43rd

REVELS, HIRAM RHODES, a Senator from Mississippi. Born on September 27, 1827; died on January 16, 1901. Elected as a Republican to the 41st Congress after Mississippi was readmitted to the union, and served from February 25, 1870, to March 3, 1871. First African American Member of Congress; first African American Senator; first African American Republican elected to Congress; first African American Member of Congress from Mississippi.

Committee Assignments	Congress
S. Education and Labor	41st
S. District of Columbia	41st

REYNOLDS, MELVIN J., a Representative from Illinois. Born on January 8, 1952. Elected as a Democrat to the 103rd and 104th Congresses; served from January 5, 1993, until his resignation on October 1, 1995.

Committee Assignments	Congress
H. Ways and Means	103rd
H. Economic and Educational Opportunities	104th

RICHARDSON, LAURA, a Representative from California. Born on April 14, 1962. Elected as a Democrat to the 110th Congress to fill the vacancy caused by the death of Representative Juanita Millender-McDonald; reelected to the 111th and 112th Congresses; has served since September 4, 2007.

Committee Assignments	Congress
H. Science and Technology	110th
H. Transportation and Infrastructure	110th-112th
H. Homeland Security	111th-112th

RICHMOND, CEDRIC L, a Representative from Louisiana. Born on September 13, 1973. Elected as a Democrat to the 112th Congress; has served since January 3, 2011.

Committee Assignments	Congress
H. Homeland Security	112th
H. Small Business	112th

RUSH, BOBBY L., a Representative from Illinois. Born on November 23, 1946. Elected as a Democrat to the 103rd through 112th Congresses; has served since January 5, 1993.

Committee Assignments	Congress
H. Banking, Finance, and Urban Affairs	103rd
H. Government Operations	103rd
H. Science, Space, and Technology	103rd
H. Commerce	104th-106th
H. Energy and Commerce	107th-112th

SAVAGE, GUS, a Representative from Illinois. Born on October 30, 1925. Elected as a Democrat to the 97th through 102nd Congresses; served from January 3, 1981, to January 3, 1993.

Committee Assignments	Congress
H. Post Office and Civil Service	97th
H. Public Works and Transportation	97th-102nd
H. Small Business	97th-102nd

SCOTT, DAVID, a Representative from Georgia. Born on June 27, 1946. Elected as a Democrat to the 108th-112th Congresses; has served since January 7, 2003.

Committee Assignments	Congress
H. Agriculture	108th-112th
H. Financial Services	108th-112th
H. Foreign Affairs	111th
H. Standards of Official Conduct	110th

SCOTT, ROBERT C., a Representative from Virginia. Born on April 30, 1947. Elected as a Democrat to the 103rd through 112th Congresses; has served since January 5, 1993.

Committee Assignments	Congress
H. Education and Labor	103rd, 110th-112th
H. Economic and Educational Opportunities	104th
H. Education and the Workforce	105th-107th, 109th
H. Judiciary	103rd-112th
H. Science, Space, and Technology	103rd
H. Select U.S. National …Concerns with the People's Republic of China	106th
H. Budget	108th, 110th-111th

SCOTT, TIM E., a Representative from South Carolina. Born on September 19, 1965. Elected as a Republican to the 112th Congress; has served since January 3, 2011. An assistant majority whip, 112th Congress.

Committee Assignments	Congress
H. Rules	112th

SEWELL, TERRYCINA "TERRI", a Representative from Alabama. Born on January 1, 1965. Elected as a Democrat to the 112th Congress; has served since January 3, 2011. A senior Democratic whip, 112th Congress.

Committee Assignments	Congress
H. Agriculture	112th
H. Science, Space and Technology	112th

SMALLS, ROBERT, a Representative from South Carolina. Born on April 5, 1839; died on February 22, 1915. Elected as a Republican to the 44th, 45th, and 47th through 49th Congresses. He served from March 4, 1875, to March 3, 1879; from July 19, 1882, to March 3, 1883, after he successfully contested the reelection of Representative George Tillman; and from March 18, 1884, to March 3, 1887, after he was elected to fill the vacancy caused by the death of Representative Edmund Mackey.

Committee Assignments	Congress
H. Agriculture	44th, 47th
H. Militia	45th
H. Manufactures	48th
H. War Claims	49th

STEWART, BENNETT M., a Representative from Illinois. Born on August 6, 1912; died on April 26, 1988. Elected as a Democrat to the 96th Congress; served from January 3, 1979, to January 3, 1981.

Committee Assignment	Congress
H. Appropriations	96th

STOKES, LOUIS, a Representative from Ohio. Born on February 23, 1925. Elected as a Democrat to the 91st through 105th Congresses; served from January 3, 1969, to January 3, 1999. First African American Member of Congress from Ohio. Chair of the Congressional Black Caucus in the 92nd and 93rd Congresses.

Committee Assignments	Congress
H. Education and Labor	91st
H. Internal Security	91st
H. Appropriations	92nd-105th
H. Budget	95th-96th
H. Standards of Official Conduct (committee chair, 97th-98th, 102nd)	96th-98th, 102nd
H. Select Assassinations (committee chair, 95th)	94th-95th
H. Select Intelligence	98th-100th
H. Select to Investigate Arms Transactions to Iran	100th

THOMPSON, BENNIE G., a Representative from Mississippi. Born on January 28, 1948. Elected as a Democrat to the 103rd Congress to fill the vacancy caused by resignation of Representative Mike Espy; reelected to the 104th through 112th Congresses; has served since April 20, 1993.

Committee Assignments	Congress
H. Agriculture	103rd-108th
H. Merchant Marine and Fisheries	103rd
H. Small Business	103rd-104th
H. Budget	105th-107th
H. Homeland Security (committee chair, 110th and 111th; ranking Member, 112th)	108th-112th

TOWNS, EDOLPHUS, a Representative from New York. Born on July 21, 1934. Elected as a Democrat to the 98th through 112th Congresses; has served since January 3, 1983. Chair of the Congressional Black Caucus in the 102nd Congress.

Committee Assignments	Congress
H. Government Operations	98th-103rd
H. Government Reform and Oversight / H. Government Reform	104th-109th
H. Oversight and Government Reform (committee chair, 111th)	110th-112th
H. Public Works and Transportation	98th-104th
H. Energy and Commerce	101st-103rd, 107th-110th, 112th
H. Commerce	104th-106th
H. Select Narcotics Abuse and Control	98th-102nd

TUCKER, WALTER R. III, a Representative from California. Born on May 28, 1957. Elected as a Democrat to the 103rd and 104th Congresses; served from January 5, 1993, until his resignation on December 15, 1995.

Committee Assignments	Congress
H. Public Works and Transportation	103rd
H. Small Business	103rd-104th
H. Transportation and Infrastructure	104th

TURNER, BENJAMIN S., a Representative from Alabama. Born on March 17, 1825; died on March 21, 1894. Elected as a Republican to the 42nd Congress; served from March 4, 1871, to March 3, 1873. First African American Member of Congress from Alabama.

Committee Assignment	Congress
H. Invalid Pensions	42nd

WALDON, ALTON R. Jr., a Representative from New York. Born on December 21, 1936. Elected as a Democrat to the 99th Congress to fill the vacancy caused by the death of Representative Joseph Addabbo; served from July 29, 1986, to January 3, 1987.

Committee Assignments	Congress
H. Education and Labor	99th
H. Small Business	99th

WALLS, JOSIAH T., a Representative from Florida. Born on December 30, 1842; died on May 5, 1905. Elected as a Republican to the 42nd through 44th Congresses; served from March 4, 1871, to January 29, 1873 (when his election was successfully contested); from March 4, 1873, to March 3, 1875; and from March 4, 1875, to April 19, 1876 (when his election was successfully contested). First African American Member of Congress from Florida.

Committee Assignments	Congress
H. Militia	42nd-43rd
H. Mileage	44th

WASHINGTON, CRAIG A., a Representative from Texas. Born on October 12, 1941. Elected as a Democrat to the 101st Congress to fill the vacancy caused by the death of Representative Mickey Leland; reelected to the 102nd and 103rd Congresses; served from December 9, 1989, to January 3, 1995.

Committee Assignments	Congress
H. Education and Labor	101st-102nd
H. Judiciary	101st-103rd
H. Energy and Commerce	103rd
H. Government Operations	103rd
H. Select Committee on Narcotics Abuse and Control	102nd

WASHINGTON, HAROLD D., a Representative from Illinois. Born on April 15, 1922; died on November 25, 1987. Elected as a Democrat to the 97th and 98th Congresses; served from January 3, 1981, to April 29, 1983, when he resigned to become mayor of Chicago.

Committee Assignments	Congress
H. Government Operations	97th
H. Education and Labor	97th-98th
H. Judiciary	97th-98th

WATERS, MAXINE, a Representative from California. Born on August 31, 1938. Elected as a Democrat to the 102nd through 112th Congresses, has served since January 3, 1991. Chair of the Congressional Black Caucus in the 105th Congress; vice chair of the Democratic Steering Committee in the 105th through 108th Congresses; a Democratic chief deputy whip in the 106th through 112th Congresses.

Committee Assignments	Congress
H. Banking, Finance, and Urban Affairs	102nd-103rd
H. Banking and Financial Services	104th-106th
H. Financial Services	107th-112th
H. Veterans Affairs	102nd-104th
H. Small Business	103rd-104th
H. Judiciary	105th-112th

WATSON, DIANE E., a Representative from California. Born on November 12, 1933. Elected as a Democrat to the 107th Congress to fill vacancy caused by the death of Representative Julian Dixon; reelected to the 108th-111th Congresses; served from June 7, 2001, to January 3, 2011. U.S. ambassador to Micronesia from 1999 to 2001.

Committee Assignments	Congress
H. International Relations	107th-109th
H. Foreign Affairs	110th-111th
H. Government Reform / H. Oversight and Government Reform	107th-111th

WATT, MELVIN L., a Representative from North Carolina. Born on August 26, 1945. Elected as a Democrat to the 103rd through 112th Congresses; has served since January 5, 1993. Chair of the Congressional Black Caucus in the 109th Congress.

Committee Assignments	Congress
H. Banking, Finance, and Urban Affairs	103rd
H. Banking and Financial Services	104th-106th
H. Financial Services	107th-112th
H. Post Office and Civil Service	103rd
H. Judiciary	103rd-112th
Jt. Economic	107th-108th

WATTS, J.C. Jr., a Representative from Oklahoma. Born on November 18, 1957. Elected as a Republican to the 104th through 107th Congresses; served from January 3, 1995, to January 3, 2003. First African American Member of Congress from Oklahoma. Chair of the House Republican Conference in the 106th through 107th Congresses.

Committee Assignments	Congress
H. Banking and Financial Services	104th
H. National Security	104th-105th
H. Transportation and Infrastructure	105th-106th
H. Armed Services	106th-107th

WEST, ALLEN B., a Representative from Florida. Born on February 7, 1961. Elected as a Republican to the 112th Congress; served from January 3, 2011, to present.

Committee Assignments	Congress
H. Armed Services	112th
H. Small Business	112th

WHEAT, ALAN D., a Representative from Missouri. Born on October 16, 1951. Elected as a Democrat to the 98th through 103rd Congresses; served from January 3, 1983, to January 3, 1995.

Committee Assignments	Congress
H. District of Columbia	98th-103rd
H. Rules	98th-103rd
H. Select Children, Youth, and Families	98th-102nd
H. Select Hunger	101st-102nd

WHITE, GEORGE H., a Representative from North Carolina. Born on December 18, 1852; died on December 28, 1918. Elected as a Republican to the 55th and 56th Congresses; served from March 4, 1897, to March 3, 1901.

Committee Assignments	Congress
H. Agriculture	55th
H. District of Columbia	55th-56th

WILSON, FREDERICA S., a Representative from Florida. Born on November 5, 1942. Elected as a Democrat to the 112th Congress; has served since January 3, 2011.

Committee Assignments	Congress
H. Foreign Affairs	112th

Committee Assignments	Congress
H. Science, Space and Technology	112th

WYNN, ALBERT R., a Representative from Maryland. Born on September 10, 1951. Elected as a Democrat to the 103rd through 110th Congresses; served from January 5, 1993, to May 31, 2008.

Committee Assignments	Congress
H. Banking, Finance, and Urban Affairs	103rd
H. Banking and Financial Services	104th
H. Foreign Affairs	103rd
H. International Relations	104th
H. Post Office and Civil Service	103rd
H. Commerce	105th-106th
H. Energy and Commerce	107th-110th

YOUNG, ANDREW, a Representative from Georgia. Born on March 12, 1932. Elected as a Democrat to the 93rd through 95th Congresses; served from January 3, 1973, to January 29, 1977, when he resigned to become U.S. ambassador to the United Nations.

Committee Assignments	Congress
H. Banking, Currency, and Housing	93rd
H. Rules	94th

Table 1. Number and Names of African American Members of Congress, by Congress

No.[a]	Chamber	Names[b]		
		112th Congress (2011-2013)		
44[c]	House	Karen Bass	Keith Ellison	Donald M. Payne, Jr.
		Sanford D. Bishop Jr.	Chaka Fattah	Charles B. Rangel
		Corrine Brown	Marcia L. Fudge	Laura Richardson
		G.K. Butterfield	Al Green	Cedric L. Richmond
		André Carson	Alcee L. Hastings	Bobby L. Rush
		Donna Christensen	Jesse L. Jackson Jr.	David Scott
		Hansen H. Clarke	Sheila Jackson Lee	Robert C. Scott
		Yvette D. Clarke	Eddie Bernice Johnson	Tim E. Scott
		William Lacy Clay Jr.	Henry (Hank) Johnson	Terrycina "Terri" Sewell
		Emanuel Cleaver II	Barbara Lee	Bennie G. Thompson
		James E. Clyburn	John Lewis	Edolphus Towns
		John Conyers Jr.	Gregory W. Meeks	Maxine Waters
		Elijah E. Cummings	Gwen Moore	Melvin L. Watt
		Danny K. Davis	Eleanor Holmes Norton	Allen B. West
		Donna F. Edwards	Donald M. Payne	Frederica S. Wilson
	Senate	None		
		111th Congress (2009-2011)		
41	House	Sanford D. Bishop Jr.	Chaka Fattah	Gwen Moore
		Corrine Brown	Marcia L. Fudge	Eleanor Holmes Norton
		G.K. Butterfield	Al Green	Donald M. Payne
		André Carson	Alcee L. Hastings	Charles B. Rangel
		Donna Christensen	Jesse L. Jackson Jr.	Laura Richardson
		Yvette D. Clarke	Sheila Jackson Lee	Bobby L. Rush
		William Lacy Clay Jr.	Eddie Bernice Johnson	David Scott
		Emanuel Cleaver II	Henry (Hank) Johnson	Robert C. Scott
		James E. Clyburn	Carolyn Cheeks Kilpatrick	Bennie G. Thompson
		John Conyers Jr.		Edolphus Towns
		Elijah E. Cummings	Barbara Lee	Maxine Waters
		Artur Davis	John Lewis	Diane E. Watson
		Danny K. Davis	Kendrick Meek	Melvin L. Watt
		Donna F. Edwards	Gregory W. Meeks	
		Keith Ellison		
1	Senate	Roland Burris		

No.[a]	Chamber	Names[b]		
110th Congress (2007-2009)				
42[d]	House	Sanford D. Bishop Jr.	Chaka Fattah	Juanita Millender-McDonald
		Corrine Brown	Marcia L. Fudge	Gwen Moore
		G.K. Butterfield	Al Green	Eleanor Holmes Norton
		André Carson	Alcee L. Hastings	Donald M. Payne
		Julia M. Carson	Jesse L. Jackson Jr.	Charles B. Rangel
		Donna Christian-Christensen	Sheila Jackson Lee	Laura Richardson
		Yvette D. Clarke	William J. Jefferson	Bobby L. Rush
		William Lacy Clay Jr.	Eddie Bernice Johnson	David Scott
		Emanuel Cleaver II	Henry (Hank) Johnson	Robert C. Scott
		James E. Clyburn	Stephanie Tubbs Jones	Bennie G. Thompson
		John Conyers Jr.	Carolyn Cheeks Kilpatrick	Edolphus Towns
		Elijah E. Cummings	Barbara Lee	Maxine Waters
		Artur Davis	John Lewis	Diane E. Watson
		Danny K. Davis	Kendrick Meek	Melvin L. Watt
		Donna F. Edwards	Gregory W. Meeks	Albert R. Wynn
		Keith Ellison		
1	Senate	Barack Obama		
109th Congress (2005-2007)				
42	House	Sanford D. Bishop Jr.	Jesse L. Jackson Jr.	Major R. Owens
		Corrine Brown	Sheila Jackson Lee	Donald M. Payne
		G.K. Butterfield	William J. Jefferson	Charles B. Rangel
		Julia M. Carson	Eddie Bernice Johnson	Bobby L. Rush
		Donna Christian-Christensen	Stephanie Tubbs Jones	David Scott
		William Lacy Clay Jr.	Carolyn Cheeks Kilpatrick	Robert C. Scott
		Emanuel Cleaver II	Barbara Lee	Bennie G. Thompson
		James E. Clyburn	John Lewis	Edolphus Towns
		John Conyers Jr.	Cynthia McKinney	Maxine Waters
		Elijah E. Cummings	Kendrick Meek	Diane E. Watson
		Artur Davis	Gregory W. Meeks	Melvin L. Watt
		Danny K. Davis	Juanita Millender-McDonald	Albert R. Wynn
		Chaka Fattah	Gwen Moore	
		Harold E. Ford Jr.	Eleanor Holmes Norton	
		Al Green		
		Alcee L. Hastings		

No.[a]	Chamber	Names[b]		
I	Senate	Barack Obama		

108th Congress (2003-2005)

No.[a]	Chamber	Names[b]		
39[e]	House	Frank W. Ballance Jr.	Jesse L. Jackson Jr.	Major R. Owens
		Sanford D. Bishop Jr.	Sheila Jackson Lee	Donald M. Payne
		G.K. Butterfield	William J. Jefferson	Charles B. Rangel
		Corrine Brown	Eddie Bernice Johnson	Bobby L. Rush
		Andre Carson	Stephanie Tubbs Jones	David Scott
		Julia M. Carson	Carolyn Cheeks Kilpatrick	Robert C. Scott
		Donna Christian-Christensen	Barbara Lee	Bennie G. Thompson
				Edolphus Towns
		William Lacy Clay Jr.	John Lewis	Maxine Waters
		James E. Clyburn	Denise Majette	Diane E. Watson
		John Conyers Jr.	Kendrick Meek	Melvin L. Watt
		Elijah E. Cummings	Gregory W. Meeks	Albert R. Wynn
		Artur Davis	Juanita Millender-McDonald	
		Danny K. Davis		
		Chaka Fattah	Eleanor Holmes Norton	
		Harold E. Ford Jr.		
		Alcee L. Hastings		
	Senate	None		

107th Congress (2001-2003)

No.[a]	Chamber	Names[b]		
39[f]	House	Sanford D. Bishop Jr.	Jesse L. Jackson Jr.	Major R. Owens
		Corrine Brown	Sheila Jackson Lee	Donald M. Payne
		Julia Carson	William J. Jefferson	Charles B. Rangel
		Donna Christian-Christensen	Eddie Bernice Johnson	Bobby L. Rush
			Stephanie Tubbs Jones	Robert C. Scott
		William Lacy Clay Jr.	Carolyn Cheeks Kilpatrick	Bennie G. Thompson
		Eva M. Clayton		Edolphus Towns
		James E. Clyburn	Barbara Lee	Maxine Waters
		John Conyers Jr.	John Lewis	Diane E. Watson
		Elijah E. Cummings	Cynthia A. McKinney	Melvin L. Watt
		Danny K. Davis	Carrie P. Meek	J.C. Watts Jr.
		Chaka Fattah	Gregory W. Meeks	Albert R. Wynn
		Harold E. Ford Jr.	Juanita Millender-McDonald	
		Alcee L. Hastings		
		Earl Hilliard	Eleanor Holmes Norton	
	Senate	None		

No.[a]	Chamber	Names[b]		
		106th Congress (1999-2001)		
39	House	Sanford D. Bishop Jr.	Alcee L. Hastings	Juanita Millender-McDonald
		Corrine Brown	Earl Hilliard	Eleanor Holmes Norton
		Julia M. Carson	Jesse L. Jackson Jr.	Major R. Owens
			Sheila Jackson Lee	Donald M. Payne
		Donna Christian-Christensen	William J. Jefferson	Charles B. Rangel
		William L. Clay Sr.	Eddie Bernice Johnson	Bobby L. Rush
		Eva M. Clayton	Stephanie Tubbs Jones	Robert C. Scott
		James E. Clyburn	Carolyn Cheeks Kilpatrick	Bennie G. Thompson
		John Conyers Jr.	Barbara Lee	Edolphus Towns
		Elijah Cummings	John Lewis	Maxine Waters
		Danny K. Davis	Cynthia A. McKinney	Melvin L. Watt
		Julian C. Dixon	Carrie P. Meek	J.C. Watts Jr.
		Chaka Fattah	Gregory W. Meeks	Albert R. Wynn
		Harold E. Ford Jr.		
	Senate	None		
		105th Congress (1997-1999)		
39[g]	House	Sanford D. Bishop Jr.	Floyd Flake	Juanita Millender-McDonald
		Corrine Brown	Harold E. Ford Jr.	Eleanor Holmes Norton
		Julia M. Carson	Alcee L. Hastings	Major R. Owens
		Donna M. Christian-Green	Earl Hilliard	Donald M. Payne
		William L. Clay Sr.	Jesse L. Jackson Jr.	Charles B. Rangel
		Eva M. Clayton	Sheila Jackson Lee	Bobby Rush
		James E. Clyburn	William J. Jefferson	Robert Scott
		John Conyers Jr.	Eddie Bernice Johnson	Louis Stokes
		Elijah Cummings	Carolyn Cheeks Kilpatrick	Bennie G. Thompson
		Danny K. Davis	Barbara Lee	Edolphus Towns
		Ronald V. Dellums	John Lewis	Maxine Waters
		Julian C. Dixon	Cynthia A. McKinney	Melvin L. Watt
		Chaka Fattah	Carrie P. Meek	J.C. Watts Jr.
			Gregory W. Meeks	Albert R. Wynn
1	Senate	Carol Moseley-Braun		
		104th Congress (1995-1997)		
40[h]	House	Sanford D. Bishop Jr.	Gary Franks	Donald M. Payne
		Corrine Brown	Victor Frazer	Charles B. Rangel
		William L. Clay Sr.	Alcee L. Hastings	Melvin J. Reynolds

No.[a]	Chamber	Names[b]		
		Eva M. Clayton	Earl F. Hilliard	Bobby L. Rush
		James E. Clyburn	Jesse L. Jackson Jr.	Robert Scott
		Barbara-Rose Collins	William J. Jefferson	Louis Stokes
		Cardiss Collins	Eddie Bernice Johnson	Bennie G. Thompson
		John Conyers Jr.	Sheila Jackson Lee	Edolphus Towns
		Elijah E. Cummings	John Lewis	Walter Tucker
		Ronald V. Dellums	Cynthia A. McKinney	Maxine Waters
		Julian C. Dixon	Carrie P. Meek	Melvin L. Watt
		Chaka Fattah	Kweisi Mfume	J.C. Watts Jr.
		Cleo Fields	Juanita Millender-McDonald	Albert R. Wynn
		Floyd H. Flake		
		Harold E. Ford Sr.	Eleanor Holmes Norton	
			Major R. Owens	
1	Senate	Carol Moseley-Braun		

103rd Congress (1993-1995)

No.[a]	Chamber	Names[b]		
39[i]	House	Sanford D. Bishop Jr.	Harold E. Ford Sr.	Melvin J. Reynolds
		Lucien Blackwell	Gary Franks	Bobby L. Rush
		Corrine Brown	Earl F. Hilliard	Robert Scott
		William L. Clay Sr.	Alcee L. Hastings	Louis Stokes
		Eva M. Clayton	William J. Jefferson	Bennie G. Thompson
		James E. Clyburn	Eddie Bernice Johnson	Edolphus Towns
		Barbara-Rose Collins	John Lewis	Walter Tucker
		Cardiss Collins	Cynthia A. McKinney	Craig Washington
		John Conyers Jr.	Carrie P. Meek	Maxine Waters
		Ronald V. Dellums	Kweisi Mfume	Melvin L. Watt
		Julian C. Dixon	Eleanor Holmes Norton	Alan D. Wheat
		Mike Espy	Major R. Owens	Albert R. Wynn
		Cleo Fields	Donald M. Payne	
		Floyd H. Flake	Charles B. Rangel	
1	Senate	Carol Moseley-Braun		

102nd Congress (1991-1993)

No.[a]	Chamber	Names[b]		
27[i]	House	Lucien Blackwell	Floyd H. Flake	Donald M. Payne
		William L. Clay Sr.	Harold E. Ford Sr.	Charles B. Rangel
		Eva M. Clayton	Gary Franks	Gus Savage
		Barbara-Rose Collins	William H. Gray III	Louis Stokes
		Cardiss Collins	Charles A. Hayes	Edolphus Towns
		John Conyers Jr.	William J. Jefferson	Craig A. Washington

No.[a]	Chamber	Names[b]		
		Ronald V. Dellums	John Lewis	Maxine Waters
		Julian C. Dixon	Kweisi Mfume	Alan D. Wheat
		Mervyn M. Dymally	Eleanor Holmes Norton	
		Mike Espy	Major R. Owens	
	Senate	None		
		101st Congress (1989-1991)		
24[k]	House	William L. Clay Sr.	Floyd H. Flake	Donald M. Payne
		Cardiss Collins	Harold E. Ford Sr.	Charles B. Rangel
		John Conyers Jr.	William H. Gray III	Gus Savage
		George Crockett	Augustus F. Hawkins	Louis Stokes
		Ronald V. Dellums	Charles A. Hayes	Edolphus Towns
		Julian C. Dixon	Mickey Leland	Craig A. Washington
		Mervyn M. Dymally	John Lewis	Alan D. Wheat
		Mike Espy	Kweisi Mfume	
		Walter E. Fauntroy	Major R. Owens	
	Senate	None		
		100th Congress (1987-1989)		
23	House	William L. Clay Sr.	Floyd H. Flake	Charles B. Rangel
		Cardiss Collins	Harold E. Ford Sr.	Gus Savage
		John Conyers Jr.	William H. Gray III	Louis Stokes
		George W. Crockett	Augustus F. Hawkins	Edolphus Towns
		Ronald V. Dellums	Charles A. Hayes	Alan D. Wheat
		Julian C. Dixon	Mickey Leland	
		Mervyn M. Dymally	John Lewis	
		Mike Espy	Kweisi Mfume	
		Walter E. Fauntroy	Major R. Owens	
	Senate	None		
		99th Congress (1985-1987)		
21	House	William L. Clay Sr.	Walter E. Fauntroy	Major R. Owens
		Cardiss Collins	Harold E. Ford Sr.	Charles B. Rangel
		John Conyers Jr.	William H. Gray III	Gus Savage
		George W. Crockett	Augustus F. Hawkins	Louis Stokes
		Ronald V. Dellums	Charles A. Hayes	Edolphus Towns
		Julian C. Dixon	Mickey Leland	Alton Waldon Jr.
		Mervyn M. Dymally	Parren J. Mitchell	Alan D. Wheat
	Senate	None		

No.[a]	Chamber	Names[b]		
		98th Congress (1983-1985)		
21[l]	House	William L. Clay Sr.	Harold E. Ford Sr.	Charles B. Rangel
		Cardiss Collins	William H. Gray III	Gus Savage
		John Conyers Jr.	Katie Hall	Louis Stokes
		George W. Crockett	Augustus F. Hawkins	Edolphus Towns
		Ronald V. Dellums	Charles A. Hayes	Harold D. Washington
		Julian C. Dixon	Mickey Leland	Alan D. Wheat
		Mervyn M. Dymally	Parren J. Mitchell	
		Walter E. Fauntroy	Major R. Owens	
	Senate	None		
		97th Congress (1981-1983)		
19	House	Shirley A. Chisholm	Mervyn M. Dymally	Parren J. Mitchell
		William L. Clay Sr.	Walter E. Fauntroy	Charles R. Rangel
		Cardiss Collins	Harold E. Ford Sr.	Gus Savage
		John Conyers Jr.	William H. Gray III	Louis Stokes
		George W. Crockett	Katie B. Hall	Harold D. Washington
		Ronald V. Dellums	Augustus F. Hawkins	
		Julian C. Dixon	Mickey Leland	
	Senate	None		
		96th Congress (1979-1981)		
17[m]	House	Shirley A. Chisholm	Charles C. Diggs Jr.	Augustus F. Hawkins
		William L. Clay Sr.	Julian C. Dixon	Mickey Leland
		Cardiss Collins	Melvin H. Evans	Parren J. Mitchell
		John Conyers Jr.	Walter E. Fauntroy	Charles B. Rangel
		George W. Crockett	Harold E. Ford Sr.	Bennett M. Stewart
		Ronald V. Dellums	William H. Gray III	Louis Stokes
	Senate	None		
		95th Congress (1977-1979)		
17	House	Yvonne B. Burke	Charles C. Diggs Jr.	Parren J. Mitchell
		Shirley A. Chisholm	Walter E. Fauntroy	Robert N.C. Nix Sr.
		William L. Clay Sr.	Harold E. Ford Sr.	Charles B. Rangel
		Cardiss Collins	Augustus F. Hawkins	Louis Stokes
		John Conyers Jr.	Barbara C. Jordan	Andrew J. Young
		Ronald V. Dellums	Ralph H. Metcalfe	
1	Senate	Edward W. Brooke		
		94th Congress (1975-1977)		
17	House	Yvonne B. Burke	Charles C. Diggs Jr.	Parren J. Mitchell

No.[a]	Chamber	Names[b]		
		Shirley A. Chisholm	Walter E. Fauntroy	Robert N.C. Nix Sr.
		William L. Clay Sr.	Harold E. Ford Sr.	Charles B. Rangel
		Cardiss Collins	Augustus F. Hawkins	Louis Stokes
		John Conyers Jr.	Barbara C. Jordan	Andrew J. Young
		Ronald V. Dellums	Ralph W. Metcalfe	
1	Senate	Edward W. Brooke		
93rd Congress (1973-1975)				
16	House	Yvonne B. Burke	Charles C. Diggs Jr.	Robert N.C. Nix Sr.
		Shirley A. Chisholm	Walter E. Fauntroy	Charles B. Rangel
		William L. Clay Sr.	Augustus F. Hawkins	Louis Stokes
		Cardiss Collins	Barbara C. Jordan	Andrew J. Young
		John Conyers Jr.	Ralph H. Metcalfe	
		Ronald V. Dellums	Parren J. Mitchell	
1	Senate	Edward W. Brooke		
92nd Congress (1971-1973)				
13	House	Shirley A. Chisholm	Charles C. Diggs Jr.	Robert N.C. Nix Sr.
		William L. Clay Sr.	Walter E. Fauntroy	Charles B. Rangel
		George W. Collins	Augustus F. Hawkins	Louis Stokes
		John Conyers Jr.	Ralph H. Metcalfe	
		Ronald V. Dellums	Parren J. Mitchell	
1	Senate	Edward W. Brooke		
91st Congress (1969-1971)				
10	House	Shirley A. Chisholm	John Conyers Jr.	Adam C. Powell Jr.
		William L. Clay Sr.	William L. Dawson	Louis Stokes
		George W. Collins	Charles C. Diggs Jr.	
		Augustus F. Hawkins	Robert N.C. Nix	
1	Senate	Edward W. Brooke		
90th Congress (1967-1969)				
5[n]	House	John Conyers Jr.	Charles C. Diggs Jr.	Robert N.C. Nix Sr.
		William L. Dawson	Augustus F. Hawkins	
1	Senate	Edward W. Brooke		
89th Congress (1965-1967)				
6	House	John Conyers Jr.	Charles Diggs Jr.	Robert N.C. Nix Sr.
		William L. Dawson	Augustus F. Hawkins	Adam Clayton Powell Jr.
	Senate	None		
88th Congress (1963-1965)				
5	House:	William L. Dawson	Augustus F. Hawkins	Adam C. Powell Jr.

No.[a]	Chamber	Names[b]		
		Charles C. Diggs Jr.	Robert N.C. Nix Sr.	
	Senate	None		
		85th - 87th Congresses (1957-1963)		
4	House	William L. Dawson	Robert N.C. Nix Sr.	
		Charles C. Diggs Jr.	Adam C. Powell Jr.	
	Senate	None		
		84th Congress (1955-1957)		
3	House	William L. Dawson	Charles C. Diggs Jr.	Adam C. Powell Jr.
		79th - 83rd Congresses (1945-1955)		
2	House	William L. Dawson	Adam C. Powell Jr.	
	Senate	None		
		78th Congress (1943-1945)		
1	House	William L. Dawson		
	Senate	None		
		74th - 77th Congresses (1935-1943)		
1	House	Arthur W. Mitchell		
	Senate	None		
		71st - 73rd Congresses (1929-1935)		
1	House	Oscar S. DePriest		
	Senate	None		
		57th - 70th Congresses (1901-1929)		
	House	None		
	Senate	None		
		55th - 56th Congresses (1897-1901)		
1	House	George H. White		
	Senate	None		
		53rd - 54th Congresses (1893-1897)		
1	House	George W. Murray		
	Senate	None		
		52nd Congress (1891-1893)		
1	House	Henry P. Cheatham		
	Senate	None		
		51st Congress (1889-1891)		
3	House	Henry P. Cheatham	John M. Langston	Thomas E. Miller
	Senate	None		
		50th Congress (1887-1889)		
	House	None		

No.[a]	Chamber	Names[b]		
	Senate	None		
48th - 49th Congresses (1883-1887)				
2	House	James E. O'Hara	Robert Smalls	
	Senate	None		
47th Congress (1881-1883)				
2	House	John R. Lynch	Robert Smalls	
	Senate	None		
46th Congress (1879-1881)				
	House	None		
1	Senate	Blanche K. Bruce		
45th Congress (1877-1879)				
3	House	Richard H. Cain	Joseph H. Rainey	Robert Smalls
1	Senate	Blanche K. Bruce		
44th Congress (1875-1877)				
7	House	Jeremiah Haralson	Charles E. Nash	Josiah T. Walls
		John A. Hyman	Joseph H. Rainey	
		John R. Lynch	Robert Smalls	
1	Senate	Blanche K. Bruce		
43rd Congress (1873-1875)				
7	House	Richard H. Cain	Joseph H. Rainey	Josiah T. Walls
		Robert B. Elliott	Alonzo J. Ransier	
		John R. Lynch	James T. Rapier	
	Senate	None		
42nd Congress (1871-1873)				
5	House	Robert C. DeLarge	Joseph H. Rainey	Josiah T. Walls
		Robert B. Elliott	Benjamin S. Turner	
	Senate	None		
41st Congress (1869-1871)[o]				
2	House	Jefferson F. Long	Joseph H. Rainey	
1	Senate	Hiram R. Revels[p]		

a. Unless otherwise specified, number given is the largest number of African Americans serving at any one time during each Congress.

b. For specific dates of service, please see each individual Member's biographical entry in this report.

c. 44 different African Americans were elected to the House in the 112th Congress; Rep. Donald Payne died in March 2012 and was replaced by his son, Donald Payne, Jr. in November 2012; Rep. Jesse Jackson Jr. resigned in November 2012.

d. Although 46 different African Americans were elected to the House in the 110th Congress, 42 was the highest number to serve at any one time. Rep. Laura Richardson filled the seat vacated by the death of Rep. Juanita Millender-McDonald; Rep. André Carson filled the seat vacated by the death of his grandmother,

Rep. Julia Carson; Rep. Donna Edwards filled the seat vacated by the resignation of Rep. Albert Wynn; and Rep. Marcia Fudge filled the seat vacated by the death of Rep. Stephanie Tubbs Jones.

e. Although 40 different African Americans were elected to the House in the 108th Congress, 39 was the largest number to serve at any one time. Rep. G.K. Butterfield filled the seat vacated by the resignation of Rep. Frank Ballance.

f. Although 40 different African Americans were elected to the House in the 107th Congress, 39 was the largest number to serve at any one time. Rep. Julian Dixon was reelected to the 107th Congress but died on Dec. 8, 2000, before the Congress commenced; his seat was filled by Rep. Diane Watson.

g. Although 41 different African Americans were elected to the House in the 105th Congress, 39 was the largest number to serve at any one time. Rep Gregory Meeks filled the seat vacated by the resignation of Rep. Floyd Flake, and Rep. Barbara Lee filled the seat vacated by the resignation of Rep. Ron Dellums.

h. Although 43 different African Americans were elected to the House in the 104th Congress, 40 was the largest number to serve at any one time. Rep. Jesse Jackson Jr. filled the seat vacated by the resignation of Rep. Mel Reynolds; Rep. Juanita Millender-McDonald filled the seat vacated by the resignation of Rep. Walter Tucker; and Rep. Elijah Cummings filled the seat vacated by the resignation of Rep. Kweisi Mfume.

i. Although 40 different African Americans were elected to the House in the 103rd Congress, 39 was the largest number to serve at any one time. Rep. Bennie Thompson filled the seat vacated by Rep. Mike Espy, who resigned to serve as Secretary of Agriculture.

j. Although 28 different African Americans were elected to the House in the 102nd Congress, 27 was the largest number to serve at any one time. Rep. Lucien Blackwell filled the seat vacated by the resignation of Rep. William H. Gray III.

k. Although 25 different African Americans were elected to the House in the 101st Congress, 24 was the largest number to serve at any one time. Rep. Craig Washington filled the seat vacated by the death of Rep. Mickey Leland.

l. Although 22 different African Americans were elected to the House in the 98th Congress, 21 was the largest number to serve at any one time. Rep. Charles Hayes filled the seat vacated by Rep. Harold Washington, who resigned to serve as Mayor of Chicago.

m. Although 18 different African Americans were elected to the House in the 96th Congress, 17 was the largest number to serve at any one time. Rep. George Crockett filled the seat vacated by the resignation of Rep. Charles Diggs Jr.

n. Rep. Adam Clayton Powell Jr. was reelected to the House in the 90th Congress, but was excluded and not seated. He was then reelected to the seat vacated by his exclusion but never took the oath of office.

o. There were no African American Members of Congress until 1870, the 41st Congress, 2nd session.

p. Seated after Mississippi was readmitted to the Union on February 23, 1870; first African American Member of Congress.

Table 2. African American Members of Congress, 41st Congress to Present, by State or Territory

Alabama (6 African-American Members)

Artur Davis	Earl F. Hilliard	Terrycina "Terri" Sewell
Jeremiah Haralson	James T. Rapier	Benjamin S. Turner

California (12 African-American Members)

Karen Bass	Mervyn M. Dymally	Laura Richardson
Yvonne Braithwaite Burke	Augustus F. Hawkins	Walter R. Tucker
Ronald V. Dellums	Barbara Lee	Maxine Waters
Julian C. Dixon	Juanita Millender-McDonald	Diane E. Watson

Connecticut (1 African-American Member)

Gary A. Franks	

District of Columbia (2 African-American Members)

Walter E. Fauntroy	Eleanor Holmes Norton

Florida (7 African-American Members)

Corrine Brown	Kendrick Meek	Frederica Wilson
Alcee L. Hastings	Josiah T. Walls	
Carrie P. Meek	Allen B. West	

Georgia (8 African-American Members)

Sanford D. Bishop Jr.	Jefferson F. Long	David Scott
Henry C. (Hank) Johnson Jr.	Denise L. Majette	Andrew J. Young
John R. Lewis	Cynthia A. McKinney	

Illinois (17 African-American Members)

Roland Burris[a]	Charles A. Hayes	Melvin J. Reynolds
Cardiss Collins	Jesse L. Jackson, Jr.	Bobby L. Rush
George W. Collins	Ralph H. Metcalfe	Gus Savage
Danny K. Davis	Arthur W. Mitchell	Bennett M. Stewart
William L. Dawson	Carol Moseley-Braun[a]	Harold D. Washington
Oscar S. DePriest	Barack Obama[a]	

Indiana (3 African-American Members)

André Carson	Julia Carson	Katie B. Hall

Louisiana (4 African-American Members)

Cleo Fields	Charles E. Nash	Cedric L. Richmond
William J. Jefferson		

Maryland (5 African-American Members)

Elijah E. Cummings	Parren J. Mitchell	Albert R. Wynn
Donna Edwards	Kweisi Mfume	

Massachusetts (1 African-American Member)		
Edward W. Brooke[a]		

Michigan (6 African-American Members)		
Hansen H. Clarke	John Conyers Jr.	Charles C. Diggs Jr.
Barbara-Rose Collins	George W. Crockett	Carolyn Cheeks Kilpatrick

Minnesota (1 African-American Member)		
Keith Ellison		

Mississippi (5 African-American Members)		
Blanche K. Bruce[a]	John R. Lynch	Bennie G. Thompson
Albert M. (Mike) Espy	Hiram Rhodes Revels[a]	

Missouri (4 African-American Members)		
William Lacy Clay Jr.	Emanuel Cleaver II	Alan D. Wheat
William L. Clay Sr.		

New Jersey (2 African-American Members)		
Donald M. Payne	Donald M. Payne Jr.	

New York (9 African-American Members)		
Shirley A. Chisholm	Gregory Meeks	Charles B. Rangel
Yvette D. Clarke	Major R. Owens	Edolphus Towns
Floyd H. Flake	Adam Clayton Powell Jr.	Alton R. Waldon Jr.

North Carolina (8 African-American Members)		
Frank W. Ballance Jr.	Eva M. Clayton	Melvin L. Watt
G.K. Butterfield	John A. Hyman	George H. White
Henry P. Cheatham	James E. O'Hara	

Ohio (3 African-American Members)		
Marcia L. Fudge	Stephanie Tubbs Jones	Louis Stokes

Oklahoma (1 African-American Member)		
J.C. Watts Jr.		

Pennsylvania (4 African-American Members)		
Lucien E. Blackwell	William H. Gray III	Robert N.C. Nix Sr.
Chaka Fattah		

South Carolina (10 African-American Members)		
Richard H. Cain	Thomas E. Miller	Tim Scott
James E. Clyburn	George W. Murray	Robert Smalls
Robert C. DeLarge	Joseph H. Rainey	
Robert B. Elliott	Alonzo J. Ransier	

Tennessee (2 African-American Members)		
Harold E. Ford Jr.	Harold E. Ford Sr.	

Texas (6 African-American Members)		
Al Green	Eddie Bernice Johnson	George T. (Mickey) Leland
Sheila Jackson Lee	Barbara C. Jordan	Craig A. Washington

Virginia (2 African-American Members)	
John M. Langston	Robert C. Scott

Virgin Islands (3 African-American Members)		
Donna M. Christensen	Melvin H. Evans	Victor O. Frazer

Wisconsin (1 African-American Member)
Gwen Moore

a.   Serves/served in the Senate.

Table 3. Number of African American Members in the U.S. Congress, 41st Congress to Present

Congress	Year	Total African American Members of Congress	African American Members of House[a]	African American Members of Senate[b]
41st	1869-1871	3	2	1
42nd	1871-1873	5	5	–
43rd	1873-1875	7	7	–
44th	1875-1877	8	7	1
45th	1877-1879	4	3	1
46th	1879-1881	1	–	1
47th	1881-1883	2	2	–
48th	1883-1885	2	2	–
49th	1885-1887	2	2	–
50th	1887-1889	–	·	–
51st	1889-1891	3	3	–
52nd	1891-1893	1	1	–
53rd	1893-1895	1	1	–
54th	1895-1897	1	1	–
55th	1897-1899	1	1	–
56th	1899-1901	1	1	–
57th	1901-1903	–	–	–
58th	1903-1905	–	–	–
59th	1905-1907	–	–	–
60th	1907-1909	–	–	–
61st	1909-1911	–	–	–
62nd	1911-1913	–	–	–
63rd	1913-1915	–	–	–
64th	1915-1917	–	–	–
65th	1917-1919	–	–	–
66th	1919-1921	–	–	–
67th	1921-1923	–	–	–
68th	1923-1925	–	–	–
69th	1925-1927	–	–	–
70th	1927-1929	–	–	–
71st	1929-1931	1	1	–
72nd	1931-1933	1	1	–
73rd	1933-1935	1	1	–
74th	1935-1937	1	1	–
75th	1937-1939	1	1	–

Congress	Year	Total African American Members of Congress	African American Members of House[a]	African American Members of Senate[b]
76th	1939-1941	1	1	–
77th	1941-1943	1	1	–
78th	1943-1945	1	1	–
79th	1945-1947	2	2	–
80th	1947-1949	2	2	–
81st	1949-1951	2	2	–
82nd	1951-1953	2	2	–
83rd	1953-1955	2	2	–
84th	1955-1957	3	3	–
85th	1957-1959	4	4	–
86th	1959-1961	4	4	–
87th	1961-1963	4	4	–
88th	1963-1965	5	5	–
89th	1965-1967	6	6	–
90th	1967-1969	6	5	1
91st	1969-1971	11	10	1
92nd	1971-1973	14	13	1
93rd	1973-1975	17	16	1
94th	1975-1977	18	17	1
95th	1977-1979	18	17	1
96th	1979-1981	17	17	–
97th	1981-1983	19	19	–
98th	1983-1985	21	21	–
99th	1985-1987	21	21	–
100th	1987-1989	23	23	–
101st	1989-1991	24	24	–
102nd	1991-1993	27	27	–
103rd	1993-1995	40	39	1
104th	1995-1997	41	40	1
105th	1997-1999	40	39	1
106th	1999-2001	39	39	0
107th	2001-2003	39	39	0
108th	2003-2005	39	39	0
109th	2005-2007	43	42	1
110th	2007-2009	42[b]	42	1[c]
111th	2009-2011	42	41	1

Congress	Year	Total African American Members of Congress	African American Members of House[a]	African American Members of Senate[b]
112th	2011-2013	44	44	0

a. The numbers here reflect the highest number of African American Members, including Delegates, to serve in the House at any one time during a Congress. For example, a record number of 47 African American Members were elected to the 110th Congress, but only 43 served at any one time during the Congress.

b. The numbers here reflect the highest number of African American Members to serve in the Senate at any one time during a Congress.

c. President Barack Obama served in the Senate in the 110th Congress until his resignation on November 16, 2008.

Author Contact Information

Jennifer E. Manning
Information Research Specialist
jmanning@crs.loc.gov, 7-7565

Colleen J. Shogan
Deputy Director and Senior Specialist
cshogan@crs.loc.gov, 7-8231

Acknowledgments

This report was originally authored by Mildred Amer, formerly a specialist in American National Government at CRS. Sarah J. Eckman authored the Congressional Black Caucus section of this report. Neal Arp II and Erin Hemlin provided research assistance and graphics support. Jared Nagel provided graphics support.